THERAPY ISN'T JUST FOR WHITE PEOPLE

Published by Lit Riot Press, LLC
Brooklyn, NY
www.litriotpress.com

Copyright © 2022 by Kiara Imani

Lit Riot Press and the logo are registered trademarks of Lit Riot Press, LLC

All rights reserved. No part of this publication may be reproduced, distributed, or transmitted in any form or by any means, including photocopying, recording, or other electronic or mechanical methods, without the prior written permission of Lit Riot Press, LLC, except in the case of brief quotations embodied in critical reviews and certain other noncommercial uses permitted by copyright law. For permission requests, please contact Lit Riot Press through www.litriotpress.com.

This is a work of creative non-fiction. The events, places, and conversations in this memoir have been recreated from memory. All the events in this memoir are true to the best of the author's memory. The names and identifying characteristics of individuals and places have been changed to maintain anonymity, some events have been compressed, and some dialogue has been recreated from memory. The views expressed in this memoir are solely those of the author.

Book and cover design by Lit Riot Press, LLC

Library of Congress Control Number: 2022932913

Publisher's Cataloging-in-Publication Data

Name: Imani, Kiara.
Title: Therapy Isn't Just For White People.
Identifiers: LCCN 2022932913 | ISBN 978-1-7351458-7-7 (pbk.) | ISBN 978-1-7351458-8-4 (hc.) | ISBN 978-1-7351458-9-1 (ebook).
Subjects: LCSH: Autobiographical memory. | Autobiography--African American Authors. | BISAC: BIOGRAPHY & AUTOBIOGRAPHY / Women | BIOGRAPHY & AUTOBIOGRAPHY / Personal Memoirs. | BIOGRAPHY & AUTOBIOGRAPHY / Cultural, Ethnic & Regional / African American & Black. | BIOGRAPHY & AUTOBIOGRAPHY / General. | YOUNG ADULT NONFICTION / General. | YOUNG ADULT NONFICTION / Biography & Autobiography / General. | YOUNG ADULT NONFICTION / Biography & Autobiography / Cultural, Ethnic & Regional. | YOUNG ADULT NONFICTION / Biography & Autobiography / Literary.
Classification: LCC PS126.I16 2022 (print) DDC 921--dc23.
LC record available at https://lccn.loc.gov/2022932913.

THERAPY
ISN'T JUST FOR WHITE PEOPLE

KIARA IMANI

LIT RIOT PRESS
BROOKLYN, NY

No one ever talks about the moment you found that you were White. Or the moment you found out you were Black. That's a profound revelation. The minute you find that out, something happens. You have to renegotiate everything. And it's a profound psychological moment.

—Toni Morrison

We find our future freedom in the healing of our past.
 —Kiara Imani

For my beloved Grandma Connie, who passed away just weeks before I finished writing this book. Thank you for loving me into existence. May your spirit live on through the stories I share about you in these pages.

TABLE OF CONTENTS

Introduction — 1

Roots — 3
- Mirrors — 5
- Not So Independent Woman — 11
- Brick City — 17
- Dear God, I'm Here — 21

You Talk Like A White Girl — 25
- The Color of Friendship — 27
- The Volume on This Bus is Astronomical — 31
- The Black Bus Stop — 37
- 5'2", Eyes of Blue — 41

The Blondest Hair — 47
- The Black Malibu Barbie — 49
- Wet-and-Wavy — 53
- Rae-Rae — 59

Black People And The White People We Love — 63
- The Great Divide — 65
- The New Free Labor — 71
- Nigga, It's About Time! — 77

Black Disprivilege — 81
- Mrs. Hart — 83
- Mrs. Wright — 87
- Black Girl, White School — 91
- The Big, White Room — 95

Black Girl, Not Magic — 103
- Whiteout — 105
- Thighs That Touch — 111
- 50 Shades of Black — 115

Love Is Not Blind — 119
- Puppy Love — 121
- Attitude Like Michelle — 125
- Lessons from Lovers — 131
- Left Field Love — 135

The Corporate Corset — 141
- White Shock — 143
- Great Expectations — 149
- Diversity is a Lifestyle — 153

White Jesus — 159
- Not my Jesus — 161
- The Prison of Belief — 167
- Modesty is a Code Word for Control — 171

Body Wars — 175
- Sophie Shorts — 177
- Put You to Bed — 183
- Cats and Dogs — 187

Death by Chocolate — 193
- I Go to UVA — 195
- Black Lives Matter — 199
- Law and Order — 205

Not So Urgent Care — 209
- Black Skin, White Coats — 211
- Silent Screams — 215
- The Song That Never Ends — 219

Gumbo And Happy Meals — 223
- Fast Food Love Affair — 225

Baked Brie	229
Bad Habits	235
Mo' Money	**239**
Rich Dad, Poor Dad	241
Monopoly Money	245
Rich Lawyer, Poor Lawyer	251
Know Your Worth	255
A Thousand Little Things	**259**
Smart for a Colored Girl	261
The Black Boiling Point	265
Letter to My Five-Year-Old Self	269
Acknowledgments	**273**
Kiara Imani	**275**

INTRODUCTION

About ten years ago, I was diagnosed with generalized anxiety disorder. My anxiety was life consuming, the type of anxiety that swallows you whole and pulls your mind in a thousand different directions, leaving you in constant fear of the future. I stayed up late worrying about things over which I had no control. I stressed out over things that hadn't happened, and I fixated on every worst-case scenario I could imagine.

Following a friend's suggestion, at twenty-seven I decided to try therapy, hoping that it would help me understand and cope with my anxiety. In the beginning I was skeptical. I didn't know any Black people who went to therapy, and most of the Black people I knew went to their church or to their pastor to help them cope with their problems.

In the Black community, and especially in religious circles, there is still a stigma about mental health care. To some Black people in the Christian church, turning to any person or place other than Jesus or the church would be considered sacrilege. As a Black woman, the stigma surrounding mental health care is further challenged by a misunderstood schema and stereotype of the strong Black woman, presenting an image of inner and outer strength.

Through a combination of therapy and Lexapro, a medication prescribed by my therapist to treat symptoms of depression and generalized anxiety, I learned how to regulate the ebbs and flows of my emotions. My perspective shifted from shaming myself for a condition I couldn't control, to viewing anxiety as an indicator of my physical, spiritual, and emotional state. I began listening to my body for the cues that preceded my anxiety attacks.

A large part of my therapeutic journey was facing unresolved feelings, unaddressed issues, and unhealed wounds. My therapist introduced me to the concepts of traumas and micro-traumas. I discovered that these traumas and micro-traumas weren't just causing my anxieties, they were coloring every aspect of my life, my relationships, my insecurities, my fears, and my dreams. Unpacking my story with my therapist allowed me to inspect, reject, and rewrite core beliefs that had previously guided me in life.

Therapy Isn't Just For White People is a series of personal narrative essays on race, gender, and identity. These essays document the types of daily traumas and micro-traumas experienced by many Black people in America, especially Black women, and the underlying effect they have on Black mental health. This book is my attempt to answer the question, "why is it so hard to be Black in America?"

The Black experience is not monolithic, but I believe that many of the stories and experiences I share in this book are reflective of the experiences of many Black people in America, again especially those of Black women. Both the telling and sharing of untold Black stories are central to understanding the pervasive race issues in America. As I share my stories, I invite you to gain a deeper understanding of the complexities of racial identity, and the ways in which they can seep into every crack, corner, and facet of Black life.

PART 1
ROOTS

I remember the exact moment I realized that I was Black. When I was five years old, my parents enrolled me in a White, Christian private school in the small town of Charlottesville, Virginia. They couldn't afford the full tuition, but between the scholarship money the school offered them and the extra money my grandparents managed to scrape up, they made a way.

Roll call at school became a stress-inducing ritual. Substitute teachers, teacher's aids, and parent volunteers would all breeze through the names on the class roster, Logan, Katie, Mark, Amy. Then they'd get to my name.

"Kai-air-uh? Am I saying that right?"

The kids in my class often giggled at the wild pronunciations.

"It's Key-are-uh," I'd respond just loud enough for them to hear, my head hanging low.

At five years old, having to teach adults how to say my name in front of the class felt traumatic. Sensing my discomfort, sometimes the adults would tell me how different, or interesting, or beautiful my name was, causing some of the kids in my class to look at me with envy. They didn't like the extra attention I received, but I couldn't understand why anyone would be envious of a name that no one could pronounce.

One afternoon, I remember asking my mom why my name was so much harder to say than the other kids in my class. My mom explained that it was because they probably weren't used to hearing Black names. I had a *Black* name. I was Black.

My dad's ancestors are descendants of African American slaves from the south. My mom's family is from Haiti. Although I went to predominately White schools, it was important to my mom and dad that I knew I was Black. As I grew older, they taught me about the Haitian revolution, Shirley Chisholm, Thurgood Marshall, Malcolm X, and other Black thought leaders who paved the way for Black people. I'd often sit impatiently with my hands in my face at the dinner table while they told me stories about protests and social movements. I didn't see the value in learning about a bunch of dead Black people.

Growing up, I wished I could tell people that I was mixed with something. White, Filipino, Puerto Rican, I wanted to be anything but just Black. But just Black was what I was, and it wasn't until my late twenties that I truly began to embrace my color and my culture. My perception of Blackness gradually shifted as I learned more about my own family history. The more I learned about my ancestors, the better I understood myself, and the better I understood myself, the easier it was to love myself. Black was not just the color of my skin, it was the story of my past.

CHAPTER 1
MIRRORS

I started going to therapy at twenty-seven years old. At the time, I had a high-powered, six-figure job, a brand-new Lexus SUV, and a chic apartment in the heart of Hollywood. Nonetheless, I was inexplicably discontent. I felt like I didn't really know myself. My accomplishments felt empty, and my desires were unclear. Some days, I couldn't even bring myself to get out of bed. I'd anxiously lie in the dark, ruminating over questions I couldn't answer.

Did I really like being a lawyer? If I weren't Black, would I have felt the same pressure to pursue a high-status position? Was I too strong and independent to be a wife? If I were lighter skinned with longer hair, would I be more desirable? If I had children one day, would they have brown skin and cotton candy hair like mine? Would the world embrace them, or fear them? My anxieties and fears were all-consuming, running through my mind on what felt like a never-ending loop.

One evening, after locking myself in my room for twenty-four hours enumerating my fears, my good friend and then roommate Kendall knocked on my door and asked if she could come in. Kendall is White and Filipino, and just one year older than me. Her soothing voice and gentle demeanor can warm even the coldest of hearts. I've always admired that about her.

Kendall is also highly intuitive and has always been the kind of friend that can tell if something is wrong just by looking in your eyes. Although I usually preferred to spiral in silence, I knew there was no point in trying to hide from Kendall. I invited her in, and she climbed into my bed. It felt good to have someone next to me.

After talking through many of my fears with Kendall she suggested that I try going to therapy. She shared with me how therapy helped her walk away from an emotionally toxic relationship and changed her life. Initially, I was skeptical. I didn't understand how talking to a stranger about my fears would help. Other than Kendall, I didn't know many people who went to therapy, and I definitely didn't know any Black people with a therapist.

I woke up the next day feeling much better, but anxiety can be unpredictable. Peace can turn to panic attacks without warning. One moment, everything is fine, but just the slightest trigger, a comment, a song, a book that I misplaced, could send me into the darkest corners of my mind. Just one week later, I found myself back in bed. Loneliness. Rejection. Shame. It was becoming clear that I didn't have the tools I needed to get better. Unable to shake my recurring feelings of anxiety and hopelessness, I decided to take Kendall's advice and seek out a therapist.

I turned to Google to find a therapist. After hours of sifting through directories and websites, I eventually stumbled across a Black female therapist named Carrie. She was young, beautiful, and according to her online profile, she was highly accomplished. She looked like someone I could go to coffee with or invite over for dinner.

If you've ever been to therapy before or even if you haven't, you may be shaking your head at my naivety, and I wouldn't blame you. I *was* naïve.

I showed up to my first therapy session with an exhaustive list of the things I wanted to discuss, my anxiety, my fears about the future, my career goals, and my love life. I explained to Carrie that I had a close, loving relationship with my family, and unlike all the therapy patients I had seen on television who spent lots of time talking about their childhood, I did not need to talk about my past. I had a great childhood with little to no family drama. My mom and dad were still married. I didn't suffer any emotional abuse as a kid, and I talked to my little sister and brother almost every day.

Carrie could have told me that in refusing to talk about my past, I was being naive. She could have given me a long, academic speech about the role of the family in psychological development. She could have told me that I wouldn't truly be able to understand myself unless I understood where I came from. But she didn't tell me any of those things. Instead, she did what she does best. She just listened.

Talking to Carrie came more easily than I expected. She felt like a familiar friend. She never made me feel like I was being judged. I felt safe with her. In my first few sessions, Carrie spent a lot of time getting to know me. I told her about my many accomplishments, and about my experience working as a young, Black female attorney in Los Angeles. I told her about recent dates that I had been on, about quarrels with friends, and about some of my conversations with coworkers. Sometimes she asked me questions about the things I told her, but mostly, she just listened.

One afternoon, I told Carrie about an argument I had with a guy I was seeing. I expressed that at the rate I was going, I feared that there was no way I was going to be married by thirty. Carrie asked me why I believed I had to be married by thirty. The question made me squirm in my seat. The answer felt obvious, and yet I struggled to articulate a response.

On most days, Carrie did more listening than she did talking, but that afternoon she continued to press me. She asked me how long my parents had been married and how they had met. I explained that my mom and dad met as undergraduate students at Cornell University and were nineteen and twenty-one years old when they married. I was born shortly after they got married.

My next-door neighbor Erin, a White clinical psychologist with twin boys whom I have grown close to over the years, once told me in a casual late-night conversation over a bottle of wine that what we believe to be true about the world is established as early as thirteen years old. The people we spend the most time with growing up have the greatest impact on how we see ourselves and the world around us. What's demonstrated for us as children subconsciously shapes what we believe to be *normal* as adults. If our parents cuss, chances are we'll cuss too. If they work all the time, we're more likely to work long hours as adults.

My time in therapy revealed that at least in my life, Erin's observations were spot on. After nearly an hour of processing my parents' relationship in one session with Carrie, I finally came to what now seems like an obvious conclusion. I put pressure on myself to get married young because my parents were married so young. I had processed my relationships with friends before, but for the first time I could see how my family structure and upbringing shaped my ideas about what a healthy relationship was.

Up until then, my beliefs about love and relationship mirrored what they had modeled for me growing up. Because I unconsciously internalized my parent's experience as normal, I hadn't ever thought to question what I believed about love. I had never even considered getting married later in life or asked myself whether or not I wanted to be married at all. This revelation challenged everything I believed about my ability to examine and think critically independent of my surroundings.

CHAPTER 2
NOT SO INDEPENDENT WOMAN

"You've always had a mind of your own, Kiki," my mom often says when she believes I'm being particularly stubborn. According to both my mom Anastasia and my dad Sanford, I started talking at just six months old. I'd smile at strangers from my stroller who would often jump back in shock when they heard me say, "Hi!" One of the very first words I learned to say was, "independent."

I didn't just love saying the word independent. I loved being independent. As a toddler, I rarely asked my parents for help. I loved doing things on my own and I often cried when my parents tried to do things for me. I wanted to feed myself, dress myself, and brush my own teeth. I wore my independence like a baby badge of honor. My parents tell me that by the time I started kindergarten my obsession with independence led me to believe that I was entirely self-made. At five years old, I was already reading and writing. When people asked me how I learned to read and write I'd respond, "I taught myself." Tying my shoes? Apparently, I taught myself that, too.

The truth was though, as independent as I was, I wasn't

self-made. I was skilled in reading and writing because my parents helped cultivate those skills in me. My rather extensive vocabulary was not just a product of my own efforts, but the result of having grown up in a home where my parents included me in mature conversations about social justice, money, and politics.

But it wasn't just language arts skills I learned from my parents. Most of what I knew and understood about the world came from them. I inherited my mom's fiery spirit and zest for life and my dad's integrity and kind heart. The way they talked, walked, and interacted with the world around them influenced me. To this day people tell me they see so much of my mom and dad in me.

After realizing in therapy with Carrie just how much my parents influenced me, it occurred to me that just as my parents had played a role in my own childhood development, they had once been children impacted by the beliefs and decisions of their own parents. Similarly, my grandparents had been impacted by the beliefs and decisions of their parents. This revelation of generational worldviews led me down a path of familial curiosity.

I decided to spend more time talking to my parents and grandparents about stories from their pasts. I asked them about their experiences, their dreams, and their failures. I talked to them about their report cards as kids, their favorite movies growing up, their first jobs, and their relationships with their siblings. The more I learned the more I wanted to know.

One night I remember sitting in bed with my dad's mom, Grandma Connie, or "Mama" as my siblings and I call her. Mama is a small woman with big brown eyes and a sizable personality. Her smile can light up a room, and her laugh is so contagious that when she laughs, everyone in the room can't help but laugh too. As a kid, I loved snuggling up next to her in bed while we watched old black and white sitcoms like *I Love*

Lucy and *Laverne and Shirley*.

On this particular evening, the mood was somber. Mama, who had recently been diagnosed with ovarian cancer, had just finished chemotherapy treatment. She was too ill to do much of anything besides talk, so I sat in the bed and listened to her tell colorful stories about when she was a little girl.

At one point, I shared with Mama that I had been doing a lot of creative writing lately and had recently ventured into the world of poetry. She smiled before she responded.

"Did you know that my mother-in-law, your great grandmother Lizzy, was a poet?" My eyes widened. I had never met my Great Grandma Lizzy, and I didn't know that anyone else in my family had been a writer. Mama told me about how Great Grandma Lizzy dreamed of writing a book of poetry. Writing was in my blood.

Apparently, I inherited my love for fur coats from Great Grandma Lizzy too. Mama told me about how one time, Great Grandma Lizzy showed up late to my dad's high school graduation on a hot summer day in the most dramatic fur coat. My dad was one of three Black kids in his class, so naturally his family was easy to pinpoint in the crowd. I giggled thinking about how confused the other parents must have been.

Great Grandma Lizzy grew up in Newark, New Jersey. Growing up she dreamed of attending college, but because she was a Black woman, she wasn't even allowed to apply. In desperate need of money to support herself, she got a job as a janitor instead. But Great Grandma Lizzy wasn't ashamed of her position. In fact, she carried herself with pride, and called herself a "maid of honor."

When the Supreme Court voted to outlaw segregation in *Brown vs. Board of Education* in 1954, making it illegal for public schools to deny admissions to students based on the color of their skin, Great Grandma Lizzy saw an opportunity. Some years later, at sixty-three years old, she enrolled in a nearby college. She graduated from Essex County Community College in 1981, but she passed away before she had the chance to earn her bachelor's degree.

The stories I heard about my Great Grandma Lizzy that night made me feel proud and confident. Although she passed away a long time ago, sometimes I feel like she's still here. Every time I put on a fur coat, or faux fur I should say since I can't bring myself to wear real fur as an animal lover, I think of Great Grandma Lizzy.

I've also learned a lot about my family's roots from my mom's mom, Grandma Claudia. I love looking at old pictures of her. Her long, thick black hair and big stylish glasses are reminiscent of a seventies movie star.

My Grandma Claudia is one of the most resilient women I've ever met. She grew up in Haiti but moved to New York at fourteen years of age. Within just a few short years, she managed to learn English, start a family, and get her education. She graduated with two master's degrees in education from Lehman College in New York City, and eventually opened her own school in New York City. When I find myself in an overwhelming situation, I often take a deep breath and ask myself the question, "What would Grandma Claudia do?"

Not long ago, I asked my Grandma Claudia about a Haitian woman named Adbaraya Toya. She told me to research her, and so I did. I learned about a group of African women known as the Dahomey Amazons.

The Dahomey Amazons were an all-female military regiment from the Kingdom of Dahomey in what is the present-day Republic of Benin. The expertly trained female fighters were notorious for their strength and combat skills.

Adbaraya Toya, a former member of the Dahomey Amazons, is celebrated as one of the bravest women in Haitian history for her influence on the enslaved people that fought for their freedom in the Haitian Revolution. Like many other

Africans, she was abducted by the French and shipped to Haiti as a slave.

Adbaraya taught Haitian revolutionaries how to fight, how to shoot, and how to throw a knife. She helped transform the enslaved people into a well-trained army. That army, led by Toussaint Louverture, defeated their French captors. As the first Black independent country with a story of a successful slave revolt, the Haitian Revolution provided a beacon of hope for enslaved African Americans in the United States.

When I think about Adbaraya Toya and the other strong women who fought for Haiti's independence, I think about my Grandma Claudia. The same strength that lived inside Adbaraya Toya and in my Grandma Claudia lives inside of me. I am not separate from or independent of the women who came before me. I am a part of them, and they are a part of me.

CHAPTER 3
BRICK CITY

Grandpa Joey, my dad's father, grew up in the projects of Newark, New Jersey, now known as Brick City. In the 1950s and '60s following the Great Depression, Newark wasn't the safest place to live for Black people. Living in a neighborhood plagued by violence and drugs, Grandpa Joey experienced much more as a kid than many adults ever experience. He lost friends to overdoses and gang violence, and saw things no child should ever witness.

As a young boy, Grandpa Joey made friends with an old, Black neighborhood drunk named Willy the Wino. When I was growing up, my grandpa often talked about how much Willy meant to him. I didn't know much about Willy, or why my grandpa seemed to care so much about him. I often rolled my eyes when he talked about Willy. The last thing I wanted to hear about was a dead old alcoholic.

One afternoon, while sitting in LA traffic on my way home from work, I saw a Black man sitting on a bench drinking what appeared to be alcohol out of a paper bag. I had never seen a picture of Willy the Wino before, but something about the way the man on the bench looked made me think of him. I gave Grandpa Joey a call.

"Can you tell me about Willy the Wino?" I asked.

Grandpa Joey happily obliged. He shared with me that Willy was a friend of his mother, my Great Grandma Lizzy. Grandpa Joey didn't have a strong father figure in his life, so Willy took my grandpa under his wing. Despite his drinking problem, Willy loved to play chess. According to my grandpa, Willy referred to chess as "the thinking man's game," and he took it upon himself to teach my grandpa how to play.

"I didn't know that," I said.

My grandpa told me about how Willy was a history buff. He taught my grandpa things he didn't learn about in public school, like Black and Native American history. His conversations with Willy sparked a thirst for knowledge in my grandpa. He read every history book he could get his hands on. By the time my grandpa was ten years old he knew the capital of every state, the name of every American President, and the location of every country on the world map.

Against all odds, Grandpa Joey graduated high school at the top of his class. Following high school, he was accepted at Central State University in Ohio. No one in his family had ever attended college before. To this day, he credits Willy with helping to mold him into the man he eventually became.

Hearing my grandpa talk about Willy that day made me feel guilty for having judged Willy without knowing anything about him. Willy wasn't just a wino. He was a Black man who chose to invest in a Black boy who needed him.

I asked my grandpa to tell me more. I wanted to know what it was like to be the first person in his family to graduate from college. Again he happily obliged.

He explained that he didn't have enough money to register for classes at Central State University, but he was determined to enroll. He rode a bus all the way from Newark, New Jersey to a small town called Xenia, Ohio, and then walked the additional 3.5 miles to the university. On the day of registration, my grandfather arrived with just fifty-three cents in his pocket.

Apparently, he wasn't the only one there that day who couldn't afford to register. When he arrived, he was met by a large group of prospective students who, like him, did not have the money they needed to register. The students formed a line in front of a small picnic table. My grandpa watched as student after student made their case to an older White man, who my grandpa assumed was a dean, as to why they should be permitted to attend the university anyway.

My grandpa told me that the older White man smoked a pipe as he listened to each student's story. While many students were sent away, others were offered registration at a discounted rate. According to my grandpa, every time the old White man decided in favor of a student, he lit his pipe and took a puff.

My grandpa knew that he'd need to make a compelling case to gain admission to the university. This wasn't quite chess, but it was a thinking man's game, so instead of pitching himself like everyone else, he just sat quietly in the back and watched. He decided that he'd have a better chance of being admitted if he had more time to plead his case.

The following day, he made an appointment with the old White man in his office. He explained that although he had no money, returning home to Newark was not an option. There was nothing there for him.

He told the old White man about the gang violence and drug war that awaited him back home and informed him that despite how he'd grown up, he'd managed to get out without having ever tried drugs or tasting alcohol. The old man with the pipe seemed intrigued. My grandpa told the man about his one-way bus ticket and three-mile hike to the University. He promised the old man that if he was admitted, he'd be willing to work to pay off his debt. As he continued to speak, the old

White man lit his pipe just as he had done with the students he admitted the day before. At that point, my grandpa smiled. He knew he was in.

My grandpa kept his promise. That first semester, he worked in the school kitchen to earn his tuition. In his spare time, he worked out with the track team. By his second semester, he earned a coveted spot on the track team and an athletic scholarship. By his fourth year, his academic performance was so impressive that he earned himself a full academic scholarship. He went on to become a well-respected anthropologist and high school history teacher in his home state of New Jersey.

Learning about my grandpa's educational quest had a profound impact on the way I saw myself. The same determination that lives inside of him, lives inside of me. On the days I feel weak and incapable, I remind myself to remember my roots. Remember where I came from.

CHAPTER 4
DEAR GOD, I'M HERE

My mother Anastasia and her sister Maria were born with light skin and naturally hazel eyes. When they were growing up people always confused them for twins. On the other hand, their baby sister Jeannette was born with deep chocolate brown skin and dark almond eyes. People often wondered if the trio had the same mother and father, but as many Black people know, melanin can be quite unpredictable. My mother and my Aunt Maria inherited my grandmother's caramel-colored skin, but my Aunt Jeannette took after my Grandpa John.

Growing up, my Grandpa John used to warn my Aunt Jeannette that her life would be harder than her light skin sisters. When she was just six years old, he explained to her that because her skin was darker than her sister's skin, people might look at her differently and judge her more harshly. He tried his best to prepare his youngest daughter for a dark world that favored white chocolate over Almond Joy.

Every word my Grandpa John spoke about her dark skin color cut Jeannette like a pocketknife. She didn't want to believe any of it. She didn't want to be different, and she didn't want a harder life. Why should she be punished for the concentration of melanin in her skin? It wasn't her fault that her skin was dark. If people had a problem with her skin color, they should take it up with God.

My Mom and my Aunt Maria were extremely protective of Jeannette, and they took it upon themselves to shield her from the cruelties of the world. They constantly reminded her she was beautiful and worthy. If anyone said anything negative about Jeannette's dark skin, they defended her. She found safety, love, and acceptance in the shelter of her sisters' love.

But there was so much more to Jeannette than her dark skin. From an early age, she had an undeniable talent. She was a remarkable singer with an incredible range, and by the time she was five years old, she was belting out ballads. She sang everywhere she went, and every time she opened her mouth to sing people stopped what they were doing to listen to her.

Jeannette's talent shielded her from the rejection and discrimination a lot of other dark-skinned women experience. In America, we are much more tolerant of dark skin when it is home to great talent. From Ray Charles to Jackie Robinson, White America has historically made exceptions for Black people who entertain them.

Jeannette's singing talent gave her opportunities and took her to places she had never imagined. In 2006, Jeannette was cast as Celie in Broadway's version of *The Color Purple*. Based on the 1982 novel by American author Alice Walker, *The Color Purple* is a coming-of-age story about a dark-skinned girl named Celie who struggles to find her identity after suffering abuse from her father, and later her husband. In the beginning Celie is timid and insecure, but by the end of the story Celie is strong, confident, and clear about who she is and who she wants to be.

I remember the first time I watched my Aunt Jeannette play the role of Celie on Broadway. As a musical theater nerd, I admired Jeannette. I snapped a picture of the billboard before the house lights dimmed so that I could put it on my MySpace and brag about my auntie's Broadway debut.

I loved the way the bright stage lights illuminated her chocolate brown skin. She commanded the attention of everyone in the theater. I once heard someone say that good art should make you feel something, but when Jeannette sang, I felt *everything*. And as she sang, I looked around the room at the facial expressions of people in the audience. Some smiled, and some cried, but none of them were devoid of emotion.

In one memorable line from the show, Celie cries, "I'm Black... but dear God, I'm here! I'm here."

My heart cried back, "I'm here too!"

PART 2
YOU TALK LIKE A WHITE GIRL

All my life, people have told me I talk like a White girl. When White people tell me this, they usually say it as if it's a compliment to which they expect me to reply, "Thank you!" As a kid, I never quite knew how to respond. Most of the time, I'd laugh it off and change the subject.

I do not subscribe to the notion that the use of proper grammar and an extensive vocabulary are synonymous with "Whiteness", or the idea that tone and inflection are indicative of color, but usually this is what people are referring to when they comment on the Whiteness of my speech. Now, when White people tell me that I talk like a White girl, I ask them exactly what Whiteness sounds like. Most of them turn red with embarrassment when they realize there's no way to answer that question without sounding racist.

Even though I've learned to communicate in ways that make White people feel comfortable, I'm also well versed in Ebonics. Ebonics, also known as African American Vernacular English (AAVE), is a language system used by many Black Americans. It is systematic and often rule-governed with its own grammar, pronunciations, and unique cultural characteristics. Like many Black people in America navigating two worlds, I've become adept at code-switching, alternating between Ebonics and what many refer to as standard American English.

In my life code-switching has not felt like a display of inauthenticity but often a survival mechanism. It was a central part of my experience as a Black American kid growing up in the south. However, it has been a source of confusion in my life as a young Black woman struggling to decipher what it means to be Black in America.

CHAPTER 5
THE COLOR OF FRIENDSHIP

I loved growing up in Charlottesville. We experienced the best parts of every season. In the fall, we went apple picking at Carter's Mountain. In the winter, we went sledding at O-Hill. In the spring, we picked honey suckles and sucked them until our lips grew tired. And in the summer, we spent our days at the pool.

I was the only Black kid in my kindergarten class. My kindergarten teacher, Ms. Lowery, was a sweet White woman who always made me feel special. She was patient and kind like Ms. Honey from *Matilda*. She winked at me every time I got an answer correct in class and told me how smart I was.

My best friends in kindergarten were two blonde girls named Grace and Kim. Grace was sweet and personable, and frequently dressed in perfectly coordinated outfits with matching hair accessories. She was playful and welcoming and always had a smile on her face. Whenever we were asked to partner up or choose a buddy, Grace was always my first choice. Although her hair was bright blonde it was slightly more textured than the other White girls in our class. I loved the way her hair, which she usually wore half up and half down, blew wildly in the wind when we played tag or hopscotch at recess.

Kim, on the other hand, was spicy and unpredictable. She knew exactly what she liked and always asked for exactly what she wanted. Her dirty blonde hair was silky and smooth like the doll in the Barbie commercials. Athletic shorts and t-shirts were her go-to, and she drank mountain dew with almost every meal. She had much older siblings and knew much more about the real world than the rest of us. I never knew what was going to come out of her mouth. In fact, she taught me my first cuss word at recess. *Damn.*

Even as a five-year-old, I knew that Grace and Kim both came from wealthy families. Their parents owned lots of big shiny cars, a stark contrast to our shared family Ford Escort. Their large country homes on the outskirts of Charlottesville looked like mansions compared to our small apartment in the center of town. And they both had bedrooms at least twice the size of the bedroom I shared with my little brother.

Outside of school, I spent a lot of time with Grace and Kim. We went swimming together, we picked fresh strawberries and honeysuckles from the bushes that decorated Charlottesville in the summer months, we sang along to Faith Hill and Tim McGraw songs at the top of our lungs and watched Mary-Kate and Ashley Olsen movies from Blockbuster on repeat.

I can't remember us ever watching a movie with Black characters, or listening to a song by a Black artist, but it didn't cross my mind back then. White was the status quo, and I identified with White American culture. I saw myself in Mary-Kate and Ashley, and in Faith Hill. I knew that I was Black, but I couldn't fully grasp what that meant.

To a child learning colors, calling Brown people Black can be quite confusing. My skin, after all, was brown, not black. Now and then, the kids in our class would ask me questions about my skin. Some of them were convinced my parents left me out in the sun too long as a baby. Others were convinced I must have just played in the mud a lot.

As we grew older, we became more aware of race. We learned about Martin Luther King Jr. and Rosa Parks during Black History Month. The White kids in my class stared awkwardly in my direction during those lessons as if they half expected me to burst into tears. More than anything I found the attention annoying. I didn't want them to think about me as being different.

In the first grade, Kim and Grace gave me a new nickname, Buckwheat, a character from *Little Rascals* best known for his frizzy hair and his often-incomprehensible speech. In other words, he was the dumb kid. I don't believe my friends had malicious intentions, but as they had subtly become more aware of the differences between us, they struggled to find a context for someone who looked like me. As far as they were concerned, Buckwheat and I were one and the same.

My parents were upset when I told them about my new nickname. "That's a racist nickname, Kiki" my mom explained. While I didn't have a deep understanding of what racist meant at that age, I knew from my parents' reaction it wasn't good. And even though I didn't like the nickname Buckwheat, I never brought it up to my friends. The last thing I wanted to do was anger them or draw more attention to my brown skin.

In the second grade, Grace, Kim, and I were obsessed with the American Girl Dolls. Grace and Kim would alternate between pretending to be Molly and Samantha, two of the most popular White dolls. They always assumed that I would play the role of Addy, the Black slave doll. I wanted to be Samantha more than anything but recognizing that Addy was the only American Girl Doll that looked like me I accepted the role as the little slave girl.

For my seventh birthday, my friend Kim's mom bought me a White Barbie Doll with long blonde hair as a birthday gift. I jumped for joy as I tore the wrapping paper from around the pink box. My parents only bought me Black Barbies. I was so excited at the prospect of finally owning a real Barbie Doll, the kind from the commercials that had pretty, silky, smooth hair like Kim's hair.

I was mortified and embarrassed when my mother asked Kim's mom to return the doll to the store later that day. She explained to Kim's mom that she didn't want me to have dolls that might cause me to idolize Eurocentric beauty standards. Kim's mom was equally embarrassed. She hadn't even considered buying me a Black Barbie doll.

Grace and I drifted apart after second grade, but Kim and I stayed close for years to come. Despite our uncomfortable moments and awkward racial interactions, they both still hold a special place in my heart. They played an important role in helping to shape my identity. I may have talked like them, walked like them, and liked the things they liked, but I wasn't like them. I was still a Black girl.

CHAPTER 6
THE VOLUME ON THIS BUS IS ASTRONOMICAL

After I finished the second grade, we moved around quite a bit as my parents navigated their careers as young professionals. We moved from Virginia to Georgia, then from Georgia to Maryland, and then from Maryland back to Virginia, all within a four-year timespan. In each of the schools I attended I was one of the few Black kids in my classes. I grew accustomed to being in White spaces and navigating interracial friendships.

The summer before my seventh-grade year we moved from Maryland to the small town of Manassas, Virginia. My mom, who was now a pediatrician, had recently finished her residency at Johns Hopkins in Baltimore, Maryland, and was recruited to work at one of the biggest pediatric offices in Manassas. She was excited about her new job and couldn't wait to start building a life in Manassas.

On the other hand, my dad was much less excited about the move. At the time, he worked as a telecommunications attorney in Washington, D.C. Manassas was not my dad's first choice. The move extended his daily commute from Manassas to D.C. to an hour each way, but he agreed to move our family to support my mom.

Like many other southern towns in the Antebellum South, I learned all about Manassas in history class. The first major battle of the American Civil War, The First Battle of Bull Run, took place in Manassas, a fact that the town still proudly boasts. The schools and roads named in honor of Confederate soldiers were constant reminders of White supremacy. People travel from near and far to visit the Civil War battlefields in Manassas. Judging by the way the town celebrated the Confederacy you would have thought the South won the war.

We moved into a beautiful, middle-class brick front home in a quiet cul-de-sac in Manassas. For the first time my parents, my younger brother, my baby sister, and I all had our own rooms. We may have been Black, but we were living in a big house just like the White people I knew growing up. We were living the White American Dream.

Like my previous schools, my new middle school was predominantly White, but unlike most of my other schools, there was a small group of cool Black kids there, too. Really cool Black kids. The kind of kids who wore Baby Phat, South Pole, and Jordan sneakers. They knew how to double-dutch and watched movies like *Friday* and *Boyz n the Hood* with their parents. They had fly cornrows and laid edges. They spoke about Black people and Black culture with pride. I envied their confidence.

I'll never forget my very first day on the bus to Metz Middle School. The White kids sat in the front of the bus. I recognized a few of them. Their parents had stopped by my family's house those first few weeks to welcome us to the neighborhood with pies and loaves of cinnamon raisin bread. One girl whom I'd had a friendly conversation about sparkly eyeshadow with on my driveway one afternoon smiled and waved at me. I smiled back.

I noticed that all the Black kids sat in the back of the bus. Instead of sitting next to the other White kids who lived in my cul-de-sac, something inside of me pushed me to walk towards the back of the bus and sit with the other Black kids. They were Black, and I was Black. That seemed like enough of a reason. They all watched me intently as I pushed through the narrow aisle and made my way to the back of the bus. I sat down in an empty seat and nervously introduced myself to everyone.

"You talk like a White girl," one of the Black boys said. And then everyone on the bus laughed.

I felt my stomach drop as I sank into my seat.

For many Black people the decisions we make about the way we wear our hair, the clothes we wear, the music we listen to, the movies we watch, and the type of language we use send messages to the world about the type of Black person we are. Something about the way I introduced myself that first day communicated that I was not Black enough.

Following the incident on the school bus I developed a deep longing to be accepted by the Black kids at school. There weren't many, and most of them sat together at lunch. I wanted to be a part of a community of people who looked like me. I knew that if I wanted to fit in with the cool Black kids, I had to learn how not to talk like a White girl.

I paid attention to the way the Black kids at school related to one another. I watched *Bring it On* on repeat, attempting to mimic the confidence and attitude of the girls from the all-Black cheer squad *The Clovers*. I studied the way they spoke and the intonation of their voices. Slowly, I began to pick up on cultural cues. I was learning how to talk like a Black girl.

I knew they accepted me the day they invited me to sit at the Black lunch table. I sat awkwardly eating the cafeteria pizza as I listened to them laugh and joke. I didn't understand most of the jokes, but I laughed anyway.

I started sitting at the Black table at least once or twice a week. The rest of the week, I sat with my White friends. While each group of friends knew the other existed, I was careful to keep them separate. I developed a dual personality. When I sat at the Black table, I was one person, but when I was with my White friends, I was someone else completely.

I became a master at code-switching, altering my language and expression depending on the audience. When my Black friends called me after school, I'd answer the phone in a monotone, "What's good?" But when my White friends called, I'd respond with a higher pitched, "Hey girl hey!"

At first, I enjoyed playing different characters, switching between them like pairs of shoes. Oddly both Black Kiara and White Kiara felt equally like the real me. I maintained my separate friend groups throughout middle and high school. I attended football games with my White friends and basketball games with my Black friends. I joined the Black step team and the White dance team. I was split between two different worlds, never free to be my full self.

A few weeks before my eighteenth birthday, one of my White friends asked whether I planned to throw a party. It was June and our graduation was just around the corner. I wished that I could throw a big party with all my friends, both Black and White, but the idea of bringing them all together made me anxious. I worried that my White friends would feel uncomfortable around my Black friends, and that my Black friends would feel like they couldn't be themselves.

More than anything, though, I was scared for my friends to see me outside of the roles they'd gotten accustomed to me playing. It was one thing for them to know that I had other friends, but it was another thing entirely for them to see me in action. What would I wear? What type of music would I play? Would I talk like a Black girl or a White one? For the first time, I resented my double life. I didn't want to be two different people. It wasn't until years later in college that I would discover the beauty of being one whole person.

CHAPTER 7
THE BLACK BUS STOP

In 2007 I began college at the University of Virginia. Founded by Thomas Jefferson in 1819, the University of Virginia, or "UVA" for short, is a predominately White university in Charlottesville, Virginia. At the time, UVA's first year class of 3,240 students was 11.2 percent Black. That meant approximately 363 of the first-year students would be Black, which was more Black students than I had ever been around at one time in my entire life.

During my first year I became friends with a group of seven other Black girls. The eight of us naturally gravitated toward one another. We sat together in the dining hall, studied together in the library, and traded secrets late into the night while snacking on gummy worms and dancing around our dorm rooms. Eventually people around the grounds came to know us as the "Superfriends".

I met Jaylen first. We had met years prior as campers at UVA's summer enrichment program. Jaylen had caramel skin, short brown hair, and a butt that was perfectly shaped like a Georgia peach. I was excited when I found out she had committed to UVA.

Then came Tatiana. I met Tatiana at a scholarship interview the summer before school started. Tatiana was a dark-skinned Nigerian with a valley girl accent. We clicked immediately and decided we would be roommates.

Jaylen, Tatiana, and I hung out together on campus on the days leading up to the first day of school. Jaylen lived in a dorm on the other side of campus than Tatiana and me, but she spent most of her time sitting on one of our beds snuggled in a blanket. The three of us talked about the boys we had left back home, our hopes for the future, and how nervous we had been to move into dorms.

On the very first day of school, my Resident Assistant held a dorm meeting to introduce all the residents to one another. That's when I met Milan, Laila, and Nina. Laila was from Washington D.C., and Milan and Nina were from Virginia like me. Superfriends had doubled in size. We were no longer a group of three, but a group of six.

Milan introduced Kayla to the group a few weeks later. She was from southern Virginia like Milan, and a member of the UVA cheerleading squad. Soon after I introduced Ivy to the crew. Ivy and I met at a dance team audition. She was a spicy Ethiopian with an impressive high kick. With eight members, Superfriends was now complete.

I loved having a group of Black female friends. After years of searching for myself in books and movies and music videos, I had finally found my tribe. We spent our nights watching reality television, lip-syncing to songs from the musical *Hairspray*, and choreographing dances to whatever hip hop songs were at the top of the Billboard charts.

Although I'd had Black friends in high school, they weren't the kinds of friends where I felt like I could really be myself. I was constantly trying to prove how Black I was, and they never hesitated to let me know when something I said, did, or wore wasn't Black enough. It wasn't like that with Superfriends. With them, I never had to prove how Black I was, or how White I wasn't. Instead, they accepted me for all of who I was.

After class one morning, Milan, Kayla, Laila and I waited to catch a bus back to dorms at a bus stop known as the "Black bus stop." The Black bus stop was a popular hangout spot for Black students on campus. It was the only place on campus where Black students were the majority.

Most days, we waited around to show off our outfits, flirt with the objects of our affection, and trade stories. The unspoken goal was to see and to be seen. I admit there were days when I had no class but still popped up at the Black bus stop.

That morning, I stood at the bus stop feeling particularly cute when a bus full of older football players pulled up. The boys filed out of the bus in their school-issued athletic gear. My heart fluttered as a few of them looked in our direction. The football players were the coolest boys on campus. If you befriended one or even better dated one, you were cool by association.

As I stood at the bus stop desperately waiting to be noticed, my phone rang. Taylor Swift's *Our Song* blasted from my backpack. As soon as I heard my ring tone, my fluttering heart froze. I braced myself for the inevitable teasing.

As I expected, a few of the boys at the bus stop laughed at what they referred to as "White music" coming from my phone, just as the Black kids on the middle school bus had laughed the day one of them told me I talked like a White girl. The song continued to play as I nervously fumbled with my phone attempting to silence the embarrassing ringtone. When I finally managed to silence my ringer, I was too mortified to look up. That's when Milan stepped in.

"Damn, I love that song!" she said, audibly enough for everyone to hear. The boys' laughs died down.

"I love it too," Kayla agreed. I smiled at them both with

gratitude.

"Never heard of it," Laila said, her lips turned up into a sly grin. We all laughed as we boarded the bus.

From Superfriends, I learned there is no one way to be Black, and there is no such thing as not being Black enough. From the yummy shades of our skin to the different textures of our hair, we were as deliciously different as any other racial group. Being proud of my Blackness means being proud of all of who I am, including my love of country music.

CHAPTER 8
5'2", EYES OF BLUE

My Dad's mother Mama and I have been close for as long as I can remember. At five feet two inches and one hundred pounds, she was a tiny Black woman with a larger-than-life afro and an even bigger personality. Although she would never admit it publicly, she often told me in secret that I was her favorite grandchild. I was her first grandchild, and she was at the hospital the day I was born. Every year on my birthday, she called me at exactly 4:26 p.m. EST, the time I was born.

For most of her life Mama lived in Newark, New Jersey. My parents were both college students living in Ithaca, New York when I was born. New Jersey was only about a four-hour drive from Ithaca, so I spent a lot of time at Mama's house as a young child. I'd sit and listen to her for hours on end as she told me made-up stories about my dolls or princesses in faraway lands. I loved listening to Mama tell stories. She'd speak in a unique voice for each character as if she were putting on a play.

Shortly after graduating from college my parents left our small apartment in New York City and moved our family to Charlottesville, Virginia. I was four years old. Although Mama lived too far away for me to visit like I used to when we lived in New York City, my parents tell me I'd frequently chat with Mama on the phone for hours. Just the sound of her voice made me smile.

During the summer months I spent weeks with my grandparents. Mama and I would lie in the bed watching reruns of some of her favorite shows, like *I Love Lucy* and *I Dream of Jeannie*. She was an amazing cook especially known for her blueberry pies. I cherish the time we spent together. She made me feel seen and loved, and to her I could do no wrong.

When I was in high school, Mama was diagnosed with cancer. Over time she became too sick to cook or travel. Her big afro thinned, and her energy level dropped. She lost the ability to perform everyday functions on her own, like taking a shower or using the restroom. Eventually, my parents moved her and my Grandpa Joey into their house in Manassas, Virginia.

I hated seeing Mama sick. She tried to hide her pain from all of us, but I could see it in her eyes. Even on her hardest days she always took time to ask about me. She wanted to hear about my day, my love life, and what new recipes I had learned.

A few years ago, I was lying in bed with Mama while visiting my parents. She had just finished a chemotherapy session and her energy was low. I snuggled up next to her in the bed and began asking her questions about when she was a little girl. An hour into our conversation I noticed a romance novel sitting on the corner of her bed with an alluring, dark-haired White woman on the cover. Like me, Mama often read books written by White authors about White people.

Looking at the White woman on the front of her book on her bed made me think about my proximity to Whiteness. I picked up the book and told Mama about how I'd been told for years that I talked like a White girl. She laughed loudly until she could barely breathe. When she finally caught her breath she said, "Well, you do!"

When we both stopped laughing, Mama told me an old story about her and my Grandpa Joey. They both grew up in Newark, New Jersey and came from poor, broken families who had struggled to make ends meet. No one in either of their families had been to college. Mama told me that from the day she gave birth to my dad, her first child, she was determined to give him and his future children a better life than what she had experienced growing up.

My grandparents had four children and they had dreams of living in the best neighborhood and sending them to the best school they could. Back then it was rare for Black families to live in affluent White neighborhoods, but my grandparents were determined to break the mold. They wanted to arm their children with cultural capital by exposing them to people who discussed things like Ernest Hemingway, The Louvre, and Ivy League Colleges.

Mama never worked an actual job for longer than a few months. In her own words, she just wasn't cut out to be a working woman. Grandpa Joey earned a decent salary as a high school history teacher, and his steady paycheck was enough to support his family. When my grandparents finally earned the means to move to a more affluent neighborhood, Mama began her search for their perfect suburban home.

Mama found a realtor in the yellow pages of the phonebook named Ben to assist her in her pursuit of her dream home. Before officially meeting one another, Mama and Ben had several conversations over the phone about what she was looking for in a home. According to Mama, Ben was an older White realtor who loved talking to my grandmother. He laughed as she told him funny stories about her children. She explained that at her young age and small size, people were often shocked to find out that she was the biological mother of four children.

At the end of every conversation, Ben would always say, "Every time I talk to you Connie, I can't help but think, 'Five Foot Two, Eyes of Blue.'" He never asked about Mama's race, but he assumed from their conversations that she was a White woman. Instead of correcting Ben she'd laugh at his comments, determined to use his erroneous assumption about her race to her advantage.

Apparently, being mistaken for White was a common occurrence for Mama. She may have grown up around all Black people, but you'd never know just by talking to her. She could mimic the tones and mannerisms of her favorite White characters on television flawlessly. To this day, I'm convinced she learned how to code-switch from watching so much TV.

When Ben finally came across an open house in a suburban neighborhood that he thought Mama might like, he sent her an address and invited her and my Grandpa Joey to meet him there. Mama and Joey graciously agreed to meet him. When she walked in Ben was shocked to see my Black grandmother at five feet two inches and eyes of chocolate brown. She looked nothing like the petite White woman with blue eyes he had expected to see.

Ben could have stopped working with my grandparents after that. Back then lots of White neighborhoods were intentionally kept all-White to make sure no one sold their home to Negroes. Doing so would be scandalous at best, and at worst, it would lower the property values of the surrounding homes in the neighborhood.

But Ben didn't walk out. Instead, he laughed about the now obviously erroneous assumption he had made about Mama's race. Ben helped my grandparents find their very first home just a few weeks later.

Talking like a White girl did not just help Mama move her family into a single-family home. She earned favor with bill collectors, delivery personnel, hospitals, and many others.

When people gave Grandpa Joey trouble over the phone, he'd have Mama call them back instead. Each time, she was met with much more respect and kindness.

Had Mama been unable to learn how to navigate successfully in a White world, her children might have missed out on many of the experiences and circumstances that contributed to their success. All four of Mama and Grandpa Joey's children earned their college degrees and went on to have successful careers.

PART 3
THE BLONDEST HAIR

Growing up, when my siblings, cousins, and I had ashy knees, wore wrinkled shirts, or had a hair out of place, our aunties sometimes told us we looked like slaves. For kids who liked to play outside as much as we did, staying neat was next to impossible. That meant more times than not, I looked like a slave.

I had an especially hard time keeping my hair neat. There are very few pictures of me as a kid with "neat-looking" hair. I didn't have long, bouncy curls like a lot of the natural hair we see in the media. My natural hair was short and puffy like a cotton ball. If you've ever tried to put soft cotton textured hair into a slick ponytail, you'll know it's not an effortless task. My ponytails flew every which way, and my baby hairs shaped my face wildly, like a small lion's mane.

Over time, I came to conflate the texture of my hair and how it naturally grows out of my head with slave hair. When I looked at my natural hair in the mirror after getting out of the shower, I'd often think to myself, "You look like a slave." I spent most of my twenties trying not to look like a slave. From chemical relaxers to weaves and everything in between, I did everything in my power to make my hair look straight and "White".

Unpacking my relationship with my hair has been a crucial part of deconstructing the beliefs I held about the superiority of Eurocentric beauty. Although hair is nothing more than a simple cosmetic concern, my kinky hair has been the source of deep sorrow and desperate prayers in my life. How I wore my hair was often a reflection of how deeply I loved or hated myself.

CHAPTER 9
THE BLACK MALIBU BARBIE

When I was a little girl, after bath time I would twist my bath towel around my head and let it hang down my back like Rapunzel. I'd look at myself in the mirror, admiring my long terry cloth locks. I loved watching it swing from side to side while I twirled around in the bathroom. If I squinted just right, the towel looked like it could be my real hair.

Donning my bath towel on my head like terry cloth hair made me feel beautiful just like my Barbies. I desperately wanted to have long, straight hair like my Barbie dolls. When I took the towel off my head however, I was forced to come to terms with reality. My real hair didn't swing like my terry cloth hair. My real hair was soft and spongy and shrank up considerably when it got wet.

Although all my Barbies were Black growing up, they all had straight long hair that looked a lot like the hair that naturally grew out of my White friends' heads. None of them had hair that looked anything like my kinky afro.

The first time I remember my mom using a blow dryer to straighten my hair I was in the third grade and it was picture day. My hair wasn't as bone straight as I wanted it to be after my mom finished blow drying it, but it was straighter than it had ever been. I loved it and so did everyone else. All of my friends and teachers could not wait to tell me how great my hair looked straight, confirming my belief that straight hair was much more preferable to nappy hair.

In the seventh grade my mom finally let me put a chemical relaxer in my hair, permanently straightening my kinks and coils.

Getting a relaxer is kind of like a sick and twisted version of the kid's game "Mercy." Hazardous chemicals saturate your hair and your scalp until you can no longer take the pain. I sat in the salon as a little girl with my hair covered in a white creamy relaxer, also known in the Black community as "creamy crack".

"Tell me when it starts to burn," the hairdresser instructed me.

I sat in the shampoo chair, my nostrils inflamed from the pungent chemicals that covered my head like a helmet. There was no use trying not to inhale. The smell was too strong.

After ten minutes my scalp burned, and it burned badly. I frantically beckoned to the stylist, who was now busy assisting another client, to come as quickly as she could. In no hurry, the stylist finished putting a woman under the dryer, then came back to the shampoo chair where I sat. She leaned my head back and submerged my scalp in the cold water flowing from the faucet. Relief.

Hair relaxers should not be left on anyone's head for too long. In his documentary *Good Hair*, Chris Rock demonstrates how sodium hydroxide, one of the main chemical ingredients in relaxers, can disintegrate an aluminum soda can in just a few hours. If left on for too long, relaxers can cause permanent damage to the scalp and hair cuticles. The longer you leave it on however, the straighter it makes your hair.

Like many women I believed the bone straight hair I walked away from the salon with that afternoon was worth the burning. I loved the way my hair blew in the wind and bounced when I walked. But I didn't just want straight hair. I wanted straight, blonde hair.

The summer before my ninth-grade year, I convinced myself that if I really wanted to be beautiful, I should have blonde hair. Blondes were portrayed as popular and desirable. Barbie had blonde hair. Marsha Brady had blonde hair. Regina George had blonde hair. Baby Spice had blonde hair. Even Beyoncé, who was Black, had blonde hair.

I knew if I asked my mother to dye my hair blonde her answer would be no. There's no way that I could tell her I desperately wanted my hair to look like the hair of the White Barbie Doll that she made me return at my seven-year-old birthday party.

Instead, I decided to wash my hair with cheap Clorox that I found on a shelf in the family laundry room. With my eyes closed, I ran the bleach through my hair in the shower. As silly as it sounds, I was confident that everyone would see my fresh new look and be hypnotized by my magical golden hair.

Clorox bleach, which is intended for deep cleaning, is full of toxic chemicals and should never be used on human hair in its raw state. As you can imagine, the Clorox I used did not turn my black hair bleach blonde. Instead, I was left with burning eyes and jarring streaks of light brown in very brittle hair.

When I stepped out of the shower, I balled at my reflection in the bathroom mirror. My hair looked terrible, like a Brillo pad with grease stains. It was no longer soft but dry and brittle like the bristles on a straw broom. I didn't look like Marsha Brady, Beyoncé, or Barbie.

CHAPTER 10
WET-AND-WAVY

Following my bleach blonde hair fiasco, I started wearing my hair in small box braids. I hadn't worn my hair in braids since I was a little girl. I wanted a style that would give my hair a break from heat tools, and I figured braids would be the easiest way to conceal my severely damaged my hair.

Ms. Sammi, an African woman who lived down the street from my family's home in Manassas, offered to braid my hair. She wasn't technically a hairdresser, but she was one of the few people I knew in town who knew how to braid afro textured hair. I spent countless hours each Saturday sitting between her legs as she braided my hair while I watched movies in an African dialect I didn't understand. On the days she braided particularly slow, I had to go back to her house on Sunday morning for her to finish my hair.

I wore box braids for most of high school. I loved how low maintenance they were. Each style lasted anywhere from two to three months. As a high school athlete who played basketball and ran track, and then quit the basketball team to join the dance team, I loved not having to worry about my hair. I didn't have to comb, brush, or detangle my hair, and I could sweat or shower without worrying that the water would ruin my style.

As much as I loved the ease of my box braids, there was still a part of me that longed for long and silky hair. I was inundated with messages from the media and popular culture that European textured hair was the most desirable. From Aaliyah to Stacy Dash, all the Black women in music videos, television shows, and movies I watched had beautiful silky long hair.

The first time I watched the music video for "Beautiful" by Snoop Dog featuring Pharrell Williams, I noticed that none of the women in the video had naturally kinky hair like mine. Every woman in video had hair that flowed down her back like Rapunzel. The message was loud and clear. Kinky hair was not beautiful. I was not beautiful.

I wanted long, flowy hair like the women in the video, but growing my hair to my butt sounded like an impossible feat. If I was lucky, I could get my hair to grow six inches in a year. I needed a shortcut to achieve the Rapunzel look I desired.

A few weeks before I started my senior year at Osbourn High School, I asked my mom to let me try a hair weave. Although my hair had grown out significantly over the past few years, it was still much shorter and a lot less silky than I wanted. My mom had never worn a hair weave before and knew little about them. Her long, chemically straightened hair flowed down her back like the women in Snoop Dog's "Beautiful" music video. To my surprise, my mom gave me permission to put a weave in my hair.

I found a Black hair salon online just fifteen minutes from our house to sew in an eighteen-inch Brazilian textured weave. I loved the way it looked and the way it felt. I stared at myself in the mirror, tossing, turning, and flipping my hair. I felt more beautiful than I ever had.

In the Black community, women who wear fake hair are often looked down upon. With a hair weave, the goal is to make it look as natural as possible by blending it effortlessly with real hair. I never let boys touch my hair in fear that they'd feel the tracks from my weave. When it rained, or if the wind blew in the wrong direction, I struggled to blend the weave in with my real hair.

I continued to weave my hair throughout college. Although I still loved the way they looked, they began to take a toll on my real hair. After years of wearing weaves, the tension from the weaves began to break my hair around the edges. As much as I loved wearing weaves, I didn't want to sacrifice the health of my natural hair again. I started searching for alternative hair styles that could make me feel just as beautiful as my hair weave.

When I started law school at twenty-two, I began experimenting with wigs. Wigs felt like the answer to my hair prayers. I could put them on and take them off whenever I pleased, which meant I didn't have to worry about the constant tension on my hair that I experienced with weaves. I could also change my look in a matter of seconds as much and as often as I wanted without a trip to the salon. I wore straight wigs, wavy wigs, black wigs, and blonde wigs.

One afternoon while on vacation in Maui with my then boyfriend Tony and a few of his friends, I wore a long, loosely curled wig on a trip to the beach. I had purchased the wig the week prior specifically for the occasion. The hair was much longer and much shinier than my own, but to the untrained eye the wet-and-wavy texture looked like it could have grown out of my head.

Tony was Hawaiian and Filipino, and the first person I ever dated who wasn't Black. I never saw myself with Tony long term, but we always had a great time together. He was a laid back, take-it-easy kind of guy who avoided serious and uncomfortable conversations. We never talked about race, or the cultural differences between us. He never asked questions about my constantly changing hairstyles, and I never felt the need to bring it up.

Beads of sweat dripped down my face underneath the hot Maui sun as we all sat together on oversized beach blankets. I was the only Black person in the group. I didn't know Tony's friends well, but everyone was kind and welcoming. One girl offered me a wine cooler, which I happily accepted. After handing me the wine cooler, she complimented my hair, calling it thick and beautiful. She told me she wished she had hair like mine.

"Thank you," I responded, tickled by the compliment. She thought the wig on my head was my hair. My *real* hair. I liked that she wanted something I had.

"It's a lot of work, let me tell you," I added.

Lies.

"I have a really great conditioner though, and that helps," I continued.

More lies.

The group decided it was time to take a swim. It's rare that I choose to swim in the ocean or in a pool. The water mattes my hair and leaves my brown skin feeling dry and looking ashy. Emerging from the water usually makes me feel like Cinderella dashing out of the ball before her carriage turns back into a pumpkin. But something changed my mind that afternoon. Whether it was because of the scorching sun or the wine cooler, I broke my no water rule and allowed myself to play in the ocean with my new friends.

At first, I had a great time playing in the water. I felt liberated. For the first time in a long time, I released the burden of being a Black woman and embraced the peace that accompanies true freedom. I wasn't worried about my hair or how ashy I'd be when I eventually got out of the water. I allowed myself to splash and play just like everyone else.

And then it happened.

An immense wave pulled me underwater. I struggled to catch my breath and fought my way to the surface. When I finally stood up, everyone gasped. My ex-boyfriend Tony burst into a hearty laugh. The wave had completely ripped off my wet-and-wavy wig. I briefly scanned the waves for my hair, but the wig was nowhere to be found.

My stomach turned like the waves that had engulfed me as I tried to imagine what everyone was thinking. I stood there in my wig cap embarrassed and humiliated. I was too ashamed to look anyone in the eye, so I kept my eyes low, scanning the water for my wig.

Eventually, my wig resurfaced. I placed the wet wig, now covered in sand, back on my head. In the moment I would rather wear a dirty wet wig than expose my natural hair. And without speaking a word to anyone, I walked back towards the shore in search of my dignity.

I learned two valuable lessons that afternoon. First, there's no greater freedom than showing up as the most honest and authentic version of yourself. And second, swimming in the ocean with a wig is risky business.

CHAPTER 11
RAE-RAE

When I was a baby my mom's best friend and honorary auntie Tonya bought me a chocolate brown baby doll. I named my new doll Rae-Rae. She wore a red jumper with puffy sleeves that were laced with white frills. Unlike my other dolls Rae-Rae did not have long silky hair or bouncy curls like Shirley Temple. Rae-Rae had very short, kinky black hair that felt a lot like the edge of a Q-Tip.

Rae-Rae was my first love. My parents have lots of old photos of me squeezing Rae-Rae with a big smile on my face. I took her everywhere I went, like a safety blanket. We played lots of games together and had elaborate tea parties. At night, she slept in the bed next to me. Rae-Rae knew all my secrets, and I knew all of hers.

As we grew older, Rae-Rae and I grew apart, as young friends often do. I stopped seeing the beauty in her and had a hard a time looking past her flaws. Her skin was too dark, and her hair was too nappy. When I was six years old, I decided that Rae-Rae was too ugly to sleep next to me every night. I threw her in my closet and buried her under a pile of old clothes. That was the last time I saw her.

It wasn't until recently that Rae-Rae crossed my mind again. I was standing in my bathroom mirror after washing and deep conditioning my natural hair. I had been wearing weaves all spring and was ready for a new style. As I detangled my wet hair in front of the mirror, I noticed a lot of knotting and breakage. I patiently worked through each tangle, trying not to panic.

My curls were extremely heat damaged from constantly straightening them to make sure they blended flawlessly with the long straight weaves I had been wearing. The more I tried to detangle my hair the more tangled it became. Panic set in. After an hour of detangling my hair was still a knotted mess. I knew I was going to have to cut it to salvage the healthy hair I had left.

Before I could change my mind, I grabbed a pair of scissors and cut the knots out of my hair. I worked carefully but swiftly, attempting to cut as little hair as possible. Of course I had to cut much more hair than I had expected. Before long kinks and curls covered the white bathroom floor.

When I finally finished cutting my hair, I set down the scissors and stared at myself in the mirror. I was in shock. It had been years since I'd seen my natural hair without my near straight, heat damaged ends. My hair was short and kinky and felt a lot like the edge of a Q-Tip. Immediately I sobbed. All I could think about as I looked in the mirror was Rae-Rae.

Rae-Rae had found her way back to me. As much as it tempted me to bury her again, I knew that it was time to face the truth. Tired of hiding from myself, I wiped my tears, wrapped a satin scarf around my head, and bent down to sweep up the piles of hair on my bathroom floor.

Call it an epiphanic moment if you will, but I challenged myself to start wearing my hair in its natural texture. I wanted to learn how to love my hair. Although I had stopped chemically straightening my hair a decade prior, I had very little experience styling my real hair. For years, I kept it hidden underneath braids, weaves, and wigs. My hair felt foreign to me.

Unsure of where to begin I turned to YouTube for guidance. It wasn't long until I found an entire community of Black women with natural hair just like me. They too struggled to style, accept, and love their natural hair. In one video, a woman with hair similar in texture to my own shared how insecure she felt when she stopped wearing weaves and wigs, but how she eventually learned to love her hair. Hearing that she had learned to love her hair made me feel even more confident that I could learn to love mine too.

For months, I watched haircare journeys and hair tutorials. I loved watching them style their curls and I attempted styles from the videos on my hair. But styling my hair was unpredictable. Some styles I attempted looked nothing like the perfectly sculpted styles I copied from my favorite hair gurus. Other styles came out even better than I expected.

The better I got to know my hair, the easier it became to love. I loved how soft it felt after a deep conditioning treatment, and how full my afro looked after I picked it out. I loved how versatile my hair was. I could rock ponytails, buns, braids, afro hawks, Bantu knots, and lots of other fun natural styles. I began to see my hair less as a burden and more like a playground, full of possibilities.

Rocking my natural hair brought with it a dose of confidence. It felt good not to worry about whether my tracks were showing, or whether my wig might be loose. People were also much more affirming of my natural hair than I expected. For decades, I believed I was not beautiful when my hair was in its natural state, but everywhere I went, people complimented me on my natural styles.

I wish I could say that at thirty-two years old I've learned to fully embrace the hair texture God gave me, but I still wear weaves and wigs when I want to change up my look or give my natural hair a break. But I no longer feel like I need to hide my natural hair.

Learning to love my hair has been a lifelong journey. Although I still feel insecure when I look in the mirror some days, I can honestly say that I love my natural hair more today than I ever have before. I'm proud to be Black, and I feel special knowing that my hair texture is so unique.

PART 4
BLACK PEOPLE AND THE WHITE PEOPLE WE LOVE

Our first heartbreaks change us and shape the ways in which we perceive the world. The person who first broke my heart was not a lover, but a fourteen-year-old White girl named Jenna Johnson. Jenna and I were close friends in middle school. We ran track together and sat next to one another in advanced algebra. But in the ninth grade, I found out from a mutual friend that she slept with the boy I liked behind my back. She never even said she was sorry.

I've had lots of close White female friends since Jenna. In fact, for nearly two decades, I fell into a cycle of befriending the same type of White girl. These girls often fetishized Black men, Black hair, the Black body, and Black culture, while simultaneously posturing themselves as superior. Once I even had a White friend tell me that she believed she was a Black man's dream.

Hollywood loves friendships like these, like Cher and Dion from *Clueless*, Zenon and Nebula from Disney's *Zenon:*

Girl of the 21st Century, or Bianca and Chastity from *10 Things I Hate About You*. In these friendships, the Black girls play the supporting role to their White leading lady. For this type of White girl, I was the perfect friend. I was Black enough to give them street credit but palatable enough for them to bring home to meet their parents.

Like my friendship with Jenna, most of these friendships ended in heartbreak. My feelings in these relationships were often disregarded. I was never allowed to be angry or sad when they hurt my feelings. When I finally mustered up the courage to express myself, they'd turn themselves into victims, demanding that I accept their apologies.

It wasn't until I started going to therapy that I realized how deeply the trauma I've experienced in my relationships with White women has affected me. If I'm honest, I still have a hard time trusting White women, and I often find myself approaching new relationships with White women with skepticism and trepidation.

I have had enough positive interactions with White women to know that all White women are not the same. I also know that interracial friendships, when stewarded with mutual respect and a willingness to see life through another's perspective, can be beautiful spaces for growth. Navigating issues of race and privilege in my friendships with White women, however, has been incredibly difficult.

CHAPTER 12
THE GREAT DIVIDE

In the summer of 2020, America was forced to come to terms with its racist past after the murder of George Floyd, a Black man, by Derek Chauvin, a White police officer with the Minneapolis Police Department. Officer Chauvin knelt on Floyd's neck as he lay face down on the pavement during the arrest. Floyd complained of breathing difficulties because of Chauvin's knee on his neck and expressed his fear of death, but Chauvin didn't let up. Bystanders begged him to lift his knee, but he ignored them too.

Eight minutes and forty-six seconds later, George Floyd was dead.

The next day, a video of the murder, which was made by Darnella Frazier, was released to the public. Whether it was because we were all stuck at home because of the Covid-19 pandemic, or because the video was so infuriating, it quickly went viral on social media. My timeline was flooded with reactions to the video.

Wait for the facts.

The facts don't matter, the officer was out of line.

The man deserved to die.
The man should still be alive.

I could barely bring myself to watch yet another video of a Black body being brutalized by the police, but I had to see for myself what had everyone so riled up.

The video was even worse than I expected. I felt sick as I looked in Chauvin's dark, soulless eyes as Floyd pleaded for his mother. This wasn't just a lapse in judgment, it was a complete disregard for Floyd's life. I was horrified.

Angered by Floyd's murder, protests broke out in cities both across the nation and abroad. Although many of the protesters identified as part of the Black Lives Matter movement, the organization of the protests was largely decentralized. Community leaders, college students, social media activists, and disgruntled citizens alike organized marches across the country. Most of the protests were peaceful, but in a handful of cities, the protests turned to riots.

The protests angered many conservatives, who believed Floyd's murder was justified. They defended Chauvin and dismissed the stark reality that Floyd's race played a role in his death. President Trump's decision to clear peaceful protesters from the streets of Washington with tear gas canisters and flash grenades didn't help. Right wing news pundits characterized the Black Lives Matter protesters as domestic terrorists. Others fueled the flames of racism with counter movements like "All Lives Matter" and "Blue Lives Matter." America was a country starkly divided, and it wasn't just Black people who were affected.

I watched children fight with their parents in videos they recorded and uploaded to YouTube, co-workers battle publicly with one another on Facebook, and romantic partners on opposite ends of the political spectrum end their relationships. A Latina friend of mine told me that Floyd's death almost destroyed her relationship with her White in-laws. She was an outspoken Black Lives Matter advocate. Her in-laws were Trump supporters. Conversations between them became so tumultuous they eventually stopped speaking all together.

As a Black woman, it was a traumatic time in my life. I cried every time I watched the video of Chauvin pinning Floyd's neck to the pavement with his knee. The hateful comments under the video hurt my stomach. People characterized him as a thug who deserved to die, insisting we were all better off without him. I wondered what Floyd might say if he were still alive to defend himself.

Although scrolling through social media was exhausting, I couldn't tear myself away. I wanted to know how everyone else was feeling and what everyone had to say. Every time I read a post from a fellow Floyd sympathizer, I felt less alone in my pain. Whenever I came upon a post defending Chauvin, I felt rage.

I unfriended a lot of people that first week after the George Floyd video was released, including childhood friends from back home, fellow church choir members, former co-workers, and most troubling, my best friend from law school. There was a part of me that felt bad for cutting people out of my life so abruptly. I prided myself on having friends across the political spectrum who were diverse in their worldviews and perspectives, but the collective lack of empathy for George Floyd felt like a stab in the back.

I tried to rationalize what would make someone think it was okay for a police officer to kill a Black man who was entitled to humane treatment and due process of law, but I could think of no just rationale. How could I be friends with people who would defend the murder of a Black man by a police force who was supposed to protect him? Ultimately, I decided I couldn't. It wasn't just a political disagreement, but a fundamental divergence in values.

I questioned whether any of the friends I let go had ever

looked at me like my life was less valuable because I was Black. Would they have defended the police if it was my brother who died that day? Or my dad? Or was my family the exception, shielded by our social status and economic achievements?

I grieved many of the friendships I lost during that time. In some cases, I realized the signs had been there all along. Some had made comments about Black people that I had found offensive in the past, but I had brushed them off in fear of being labeled too woke or too sensitive.

> *Black people in this country have it easy.*
> *Black people are always looking for a way to play the Black card.*
> *Black people are ghetto.*

I replayed old conversations in my head on repeat, and I beat myself up for not speaking up sooner.

Other friends were opinionated and outspoken about things like climate change and sustainable fashion, but conveniently silent whenever any social justice issues were at the forefront. The silence was just as hurtful as the offensive comments. It made me feel unseen and disregarded.

Not all of my White friends jumped on the Blue Lives Matter train. Some took to social media to show their support for the Black community. They posted black squares on their Instagram pages to support Black Lives Matter, posted long statuses on social media to support George Floyd and his family, and called out other White people for their defense of Derek Chauvin and the Minneapolis police.

Many of them reached out to me personally to let me know how deeply Floyd's death affected them. Although I greatly appreciated all the support, the attention I received from White people determined to be good allies was at times overwhelming. My phone was overrun with calls, texts, and messages from White friends, some of whom I hadn't spoken to in over a decade, asking me what they could do to show support for the Black community, or where they could donate money to help stop racism. I spent countless hours on social media and on the phone answering questions about American history, slavery, systematic legal oppression, discrimination, and unconscious bias.

I didn't know how to feel as I listened to some of my friends pour out their hearts, apologizing for the sins of their racist White ancestors and the privilege they wielded. Part of me was thankful for the compassion they showed me, but another part of me felt awkward and uncomfortable. I didn't want my White friends to feel guilty for being White. In the same way that I never asked to be born with Black skin, none of them asked to be born White.

I had two friends spontaneously send me Venmo payments the week after the release of the George Floyd video. One friend sent $10 with a note attached encouraging me to use the money to do something nice for myself. The other sent $50 to thank me for taking the time to educate White people. Initially, I wasn't sure how to respond to either, so I just settled for "thank you."

While talking to a few of my Black friends months later about the money that unexpectedly appeared in my Venmo account that week, I discovered I wasn't the only one. Many of them received payments from White friends, too. We surmised that White guilt may have motivated the payments. Perhaps sending money to their Black friends made them feel better about being White. Or maybe it was their way of personally contributing to reparations. None of us knew for sure.

I often think back to the week following George Floyd's death. At the time, I didn't know how much it would affect me. I didn't know that it would cause me to reexamine my relationships with the White people in my life. I didn't know that it would bring up old feelings of insecurity and racial inferiority.

And I didn't know that over a year later, I'd still be processing through his death and the events that followed with my therapist.

CHAPTER 13
THE NEW FREE LABOR

Shortly after the death of George Floyd, I posted a video on social media poking fun at the exhaustion of arguing with well-intentioned White people who maintained that racism would go away if only Black people would stop talking about race. In the video, I attempted to explain to a White woman on the internet how racism continues to affect Black people in America. I listed several statistics that illustrated the many ways in which Black people are still disadvantaged in the United States.

The video went viral on TikTok, amassing almost half a million views in just a few days. I received lots of messages from Black youth in solidarity, who, like me, were tired of arguing about race with White people. Encouraged by the overwhelming positive response on TikTok, I decided to post the video on Instagram as well.

As on TikTok, my Black Instagram friends could relate to my frustration. My White friends, however, were not nearly as publicly supportive. I noticed that very few of them liked or commented on the video. I assumed that as White people they were simply too afraid to engage in a conversation about race in fear of saying the wrong thing.

Later that evening, a White female friend, Sydney, who had a question about the video I posted, approached me.

"Why did you specifically single out White women in your Instagram video earlier?" she asked.

I was taken aback by her question. My friend Sydney was also from Virginia. We had great conversations about music, faith, fashion, coffee, and how often we should water our plants, but we had never really talked about race before. I paused for a moment, considering how to respond to her question.

I explained to Sydney that in my experience, it was almost always White women who asked me to prove that White privilege exists, or who challenged my assertion that racism was real. Although I had similar conversations with White men too, it was generally White women who challenged me publicly.

Sydney expressed that while she believed racism was real, she didn't understand why White people were always singled out as being privileged. As a White person who worked hard for everything she had and didn't consider herself to be racist, she didn't like being associated with privileged White people.

Sometimes I fear that White people interpret any criticism of racism, White privilege, or White supremacy by a Black person as a criticism of all White people. I do not believe all White people are bad people. In fact, I believed Sydney, like many other White people, was a good person.

Sydney was kind to everyone and always had a smile on her face. She was honest and loyal, and always willing to lend a helping hand to someone in need. But being a good White person did not mean that she wasn't a privileged White person. Sydney appeared to believe that because she wasn't overtly racist, she was not part of the problem. That was not only an erroneous belief, but a dangerous one.

Like Sydney, many White people have strong visceral

reactions to the idea of White privilege. For some, it evokes strong feelings of White guilt as they think about the horrific things that White people have done over the course of American history. For others, the word privilege is a triggering word. Many believe the word carries an assumption that White people do not struggle or work hard. As a result, it can be very hard to have conversations with White people about the effects of White privilege and racial bias.

I did my best to explain my own views about White privilege to Sydney. White privilege is not something that can be earned or discarded. White privilege is a collection of benefits that White people in America receive simply because they were born White. It is not tied to their character or their intent, but to the color of their skin, their facial features, and the texture of their hair.

White privilege refers to societal privilege that benefits White people over non-White people. But it is not an assumption that all White people have an easy life. Life is hard for everyone, but people of color must deal with additional, everyday stressors that effect our mental health, our self-image, our opportunities, and sometimes our lifespans.

I listed examples of White privilege in America for Sydney. I explained that the terms "flesh toned" and "nude" are baseline colors that reflect White skin tones. Americans of all colors are required to read books written primarily by and about White people. Unlike naturally kinky hair, White people's natural hair texture is not generally considered inappropriate in professional settings. White people can easily buy posters, postcards, picture books, greeting cards, dolls, toys and children's toys featuring people who look like them.

For the most part, White people in America know where their ancestors came from, because they weren't enslaved and stolen from their homeland. When we learn about American history and the violence and destruction committed by White people, like the murder and displacement of Native Americans, the White people are portrayed as heroes or revolutionaries. When White people carry a gun, people often assume it's for "protection", not for committing crimes.

I made it clear to Sydney that I am not angry at White people for their inherent privilege. However, I am angry at what I refer to as my Black *disprivilege*.

White privilege is at the heart of the White experience. Black disprivilege gets to the heart of the racial trauma that Black people experience every day. Black disprivilege begins at an early age. For example, as described in a 2016 research report by the Yale Child Study Center and reported in Yale News, Black disprivilege is reflected in the subconscious bias that tells preschool teachers to watch out for little Black boys because they are troublemakers.

Black disprivilege results in the adultification of both Black boys and Black girls. For example, research published in 2014 by the American Psychological Association showed that Black boys are seen as older than they actually are, and they are prematurely perceived as responsible for their actions, whereas their White peers receive the beneficial assumption of childlike innocence.

For Black girls, research published by Georgetown Law's Center on Poverty and Inequality in 2019 showed that adultification, "a gendered racial bias against Black girls," is a stereotype that results in adults viewing Black girls as less innocent and more adult-like than their White peers. Adultification bias is also linked to harsher treatment and higher standards for Black girls in school, and to teachers treating Black girls in developmentally inappropriate ways.

In the words of author Ibram X. Kendi, "The opposite of racist isn't 'not racist.' It is 'anti-racist.'" *Not* being a racist is *not* enough to effect change. Instead, White people must learn to be anti-racist, which requires "persistent self-awareness, constant self-criticism, and regular self-examination."

Although Sydney did not consider herself to be racist, I challenged Sydney to consider what it would mean to be anti-racist. After an hour of emotionally draining conversation, I believe she had a better understanding of my perspective as a Black woman. I also had a better understanding of why my video triggered her. She wanted to make sure I didn't see her as a bad or racist person because of her White skin.

I was happy that Sydney and I could have a productive conversation, but a part of me was frustrated by the fact that we had to have the conversation at all. The point of my initial video had been to bring awareness to the reality of racial exhaustion, and here I was, exhausted after another conversation about race with a White woman.

I chose to engage in conversation with Sydney because I loved her. As her friend, I wanted her to have a better understanding of my experiences as a Black woman in America. However, I do not believe that our job as Black people is to expend copious amounts of time and energy teaching White people about race at the expense of our own mental health. As Black people we have a responsibility to ourselves to walk away from conversations that we are not emotionally equipped or compensated to carry. We are no longer free laborers who should feel obligated to share our knowledge, skills, or experiences on demand. Anything we choose to share or give away is a gift and should be treated as such.

CHAPTER 14
NIGGA, IT'S ABOUT TIME!

One evening, my friend Tina invited me over to her house for dinner. She lived in an apartment with her son about five miles down the road from my house in Pasadena, California. It had been a long since I'd seen Tina, so I graciously accepted her invitation.

Tina and I met shortly after I moved to Los Angeles. We had a similar sense of humor, and we often spent hours together cracking jokes and laughing at ridiculous memes. Tina was tough on the outside, but she was also incredibly thoughtful. She was a great listener and always gave me the most endearing gifts.

Tina was White, but she had a lot of Black friends growing up. Most of her girlfriends and all of her ex-boyfriends were Black. She loved all things Black, from hip-hop music to Black television. She was constantly sending me new music and telling me what shows I needed to watch. She often rocked braids and cornrows like Black girls and spoke fluent Ebonics.

Unlike some of the other White friends I've had over the course of my life, Tina's relationship with Black culture never felt like a weird obsession or an uncomfortable fetish. I always felt like she was being her authentic self. She cared about Black people and Black lives. She hated to see people suffer and was outspoken about racial injustice. She often spent her free time volunteering on Skid Row, an impoverished area in downtown Los Angeles with one of the largest homeless populations in the United States, most of whom are Black.

I never felt like I had to mitigate or soften my conversations with Tina. It was easy to talk to her about things like racism and White privilege. I didn't have to shrink myself to make her feel comfortable or coddle her in conversation as I often do when talking to other White people about race. I felt free with Tina, and I gave her space to be free with me.

I was excited to have dinner with Tina. I couldn't wait to tell her all about how I'd recently left my corporate America job to pursue my writing full time. She believed in me wholeheartedly, sometimes more than I believed in myself. I knew she'd be supportive of my decision.

"I finally quit my job," I told Tina after we'd had a few glasses of wine.

"Nigga, it's about time!" Tina responded seemingly without thought as she lifted her glass of wine in the air in celebration. The word nigga rolled off her tongue as if she'd been saying the word her whole life.

Tina and I had been friends for years, but I had never heard her use the word nigga before. At once my mind was flooded with thoughts. Why would she say nigga? Was she drunk? Was this something she said all the time? I wondered if Tina fully understood the violent history and pain associated with that word? Slavery, lynching, Jim Crow.

There is an unwritten very short list of things that White people in America are not allowed to say. At the top of the list is nigga. As Black people, we're often asked to make tough decisions when we're in spaces with White people who don't follow the rules. We can choose to call them out and risk being labeled as a militant Black person who takes everything too seriously, or we can suck it up and let it slide. Initially with Tina, I wasn't sure which path to take.

I took solace in the fact that Tina had said the word "nigga" with an "a" and not "nigger" with an "er." Although the distinction is slight, that detail mattered. In America, as well as in many other countries around the world, the word nigger is clearly established as a racial slur used to refer to Black people. However, the word nigga has been reclaimed by many Black people as a term of endearment. Practically all the rap songs that Tina listened to contain the word nigga.

I also thought about my own use of the word nigga. I frequently used the word in casual conversation with my Black friends. Because I was so comfortable with Tina, sometimes I used the word around her as well. I had never considered how I'd feel if she used the word back. Was it really fair for me to take offense over her use of the word when I used it too?

After a few seconds of processing, I took a deep breath, and rose my glass of wine in the air.

"Cheers" I responded, before taking a big gulp of my wine.

The truth is Tina's use of the word nigga didn't offend me. Tina was my friend, and she was happy for me. I had never known her to be racist, and I didn't believe she meant any harm. She didn't see me as some nigger. She saw me as her nigga. Problematic as it may have been, I decided it was okay. After all, I loved her. She was my nigga, too.

Although I wasn't offended by Tina's use of the word nigga, I still felt like I was supposed to be. I felt somewhat guilty for not feeling more outraged. I wondered what my Black friends would think if they knew I let a White person get away with saying the word nigga. They would surely have my Black card revoked.

I was taught that White people are never allowed to say

the word nigga any under any circumstance. It's a well-understood rule in the Black community that if you hear a White person say nigga, you are obligated to immediately let them know they're out of line.

Although the word nigga doesn't offend me in and of itself, there are certain types of White people whose use of the word deeply offends me. White people who refuse to acknowledge that Black lives matter, who refer to Black men as thugs, or who capitalize off Black culture while disregarding all the issues and prejudices facing the Black community, all fall into the bucket of White people whose use of the word makes me irate. When it comes to everyone else, I am willing to evaluate their use of the word on a case-by-case basis.

While I decided not to make a big deal about Tina's use of the word nigga, I advise White people that if they're considering using the word, it's wise to err on the side of caution by choosing not to use it all. Even if they've been around Black people who have let them get away with using the word in the past, it's unwise to assume that every Black person will be okay with their use of the word. For some Black people, and understandably so, the word nigga is a fighting word even if they love you.

PART 5
BLACK DISPRIVILEGE

In my experience, White people often have a difficult time talking about White privilege with Black people. Their body posture tenses up, their lips tighten, and their cheeks flush. They become defensive, listing all the Black people in their lives to prove they are good White people.

I've had many White people, like my friend Sydney, assume that I am angry at them for their being White and for having privilege, but I am not angry that White people have privilege. They have no more control over the skin color they were born with than Black people have with their own skin color.

However, I am angry at what I refer to as my Black disprivilege. If White privilege is a collection of advantages that White people have based on the premise that Whiteness is the unquestioned ideal, then Black disprivilege is a collection of stigmas and disadvantages that Black people have accumulated from the pervasive and systemic racism that America was founded upon.

My family and I have all experienced Black disprivilege at

different times in our lives. Each time its equal parts humiliating and infuriating. I have spent a great deal of time as an adult unpacking Black disprivilege and the affect it's had both on myself and on the Black people I love.

CHAPTER 15
MRS. HART

My siblings and I refer to ourselves as "The Big Three" like the siblings from the drama television series *This is Us*. We talk to one another almost every day, about everything. I'm the oldest of the three of us. According to my parents, I've always loved being the big sister.

My brother Johnathan is two years younger than me and is one of the most personable people I've ever met. Johnathan can get along with just about anyone. His big, almond eyes, bright smile, and bold laugh are contagious. People can't help but to smile back at him when they're in his presence.

My baby sister Nia is a full decade younger than me, but people still mistake us for twins. Just like me, she's passionate about everything and has always been socially conscious. In elementary school, she used to get in debates with the much older kids on the bus about the shortfalls of the U.S. democratic process.

My parents love to tell stories about my siblings and I when we were growing up. They tell stories about how, as a kid, I used to write business proposals for my parents to negotiate my punishment when I got in trouble. They talk about the time Nia got lost on a family trip to Africa. They also love telling the story about how at five years old, Johnathan stayed up all night on a long family road trip as my dad drove because he wanted to practice for when he had a family of his own. One of my mom's absolute favorite stories to tell, however, is the story of my brother Johnathan's first grade teacher, Mrs. Hart.

In 1997, my family left Virginia and moved to Atlanta, Georgia, after my dad was offered a position at a prestigious law firm downtown. They enrolled my baby brother and me at the esteemed Sarah Smith Elementary in Buckhead, an affluent neighborhood in uptown Atlanta. Most of the kids we went to school with came from well-to-do White families. The kids in my third-grade class wore school uniforms, spoke French, and ate cucumber sandwiches for lunch instead of the bologna and American cheese sandwiches I was used to.

On the first day of school, Johnathan's first grade teacher, Mrs. Hart, gave the class a coloring assignment. At the top of the assignment, the directions instructed the kids to color different pieces of the illustration below using certain colors. Johnathan, who was the only Black boy in his class, didn't read nearly as well as the first graders at the Sarah Smith school.

Johnathan didn't understand the directions at the top of the page, and Mrs. Hart didn't take the time to explain. He ignored the directions and colored in the illustration as he saw fit. My little brother had terrible penmanship, and usually struggled to color inside the lines. However, that day he was determined to color as pretty a picture as possible for his new teacher. According to my mom, it was the best she'd ever seen him color.

When my parents opened my brother's folder that night and found his colorful masterpiece, there was a big, sad face drawn at the top of the paper. They also found a second version of the assignment in his folder. On the second version, Johnathan had colored everything in correctly, but the coloring was outside of the lines and half-heartedly done. My mother asked him what had happened.

Johnathan lowered his head. He explained that Mrs. Hart made him re-do his assignment because he used the wrong colors the first time. She also told him that he needed to go back to kindergarten.

My parents were fuming. They couldn't believe that a teacher would say something like that to a child on the first day of school. Mrs. Hart had not only assumed that Johnathan was not as smart as his classmates, but that there was no possible way he'd be able to catch up to his White peers. Immediately, my mother scheduled a meeting to talk to Mrs. Hart and the principal of our new school.

If you've never seen my mother mad, picture a Category 5 hurricane, raging and relentless. She walked into the classroom the next afternoon and let Mrs. Hart have it. She told her that she had better never say something like that to her son again. She made it clear that if Mrs. Hart had an issue with Johnathan's academic performance, she needed to talk to his parents.

My mom took the following week off from work to teach Johnathan how to read. They used flashcards and workbooks and played reading games together. Johnathan was an exceptionally fast learner. That week, she took every opportunity to speak words of affirmation to him and to remind him how intelligent he was. And he believed her.

Before long, my brother Johnathan was the best reader in his class. By the end of the year he had more accelerated reading points in a popular reading program used by the school to test reading comprehension than any other kid in the entire grade. When Johnathan graduated from fifth grade at his elementary school in Manassas, Virginia years later, he was reading at an eleventh-grade level. To this day he holds the record for the most books read in one year.

Johnathan went on to graduate from medical school at Wake Forest University where he served as the president of his class. When he graduated, he joined the pediatric residency program at Columbia Hospital. He still loves to read, and when he's not at the hospital, he reads every chance he gets.

Intelligent, creative, and passionate little boys of color like my little brother Johnathan slip through the cracks every day. Thanks to Mrs. Hart, he could have grown up believing he wasn't smart enough to become a doctor. It scares me to think about what might have happened to Johnathan if he didn't have parents who advocated for him in the classroom every step of the way.

CHAPTER 16
MRS. WRIGHT

My family moved a lot when I was younger. We moved from New York to Virginia, then to Georgia, on to Maryland, and then back to Virginia. At each school, I was placed into the gifted and talented program. I was almost always the only Black kid in these programs. Occasionally, I found myself in a class with Asian and Indian students, but most of the students were White. All my teachers were White too. Eventually I came to believe that White people must just be smarter than everyone else.

In the fifth grade I attended a school called Talbot Springs in Columbia, Maryland. Although the school was predominately White like my prior schools, I had one of my first Black teachers, Mrs. Wright, who taught advanced math. She was confident, kind, and as far as I was concerned, a math genius. I had never known what it was like to have a teacher who looked like me. I saw myself in her textured hair and in her cinnamon brown skin. I loved watching her command the classroom. I couldn't believe that my White peers got to experience having teachers who looked like them all the time.

Mrs. Wright challenged everything I believed about the intellectual superiority of White people. I knew that my mom and dad were smart, but as far as I was concerned my parents weren't the rule but the exception. My mom graduated from a prestigious magnet high school in New York City named Bronx Science. My dad graduated from Newark Academy in New Jersey at just fifteen years old. Until I met Mrs. Wright, I had never imagined that I'd have a Black teacher who was smart just like my parents.

Besides being a great role model, Mrs. Wright was an advocate for my academic growth and development. A few weeks into school she encouraged me to run for a student council position as a representative of my fifth-grade homeroom class.

"You are a leader," she insisted. "I believe in you. And I believe your classmates will too."

She was right. My classmates chose me to represent them on the student council. As a member of the student council, I was invited to visit Washington D.C. with the other student council members. We learned about the American political process, visited the Washington Monument, and toured the Senate building. My position on the student council was the first of many leadership positions I held over the course of my educational career from elementary school through law school.

After the fifth grade, I didn't have any other Black female teachers until college. At the beginning of each school year I'd look at my list of teachers in anticipation, only to be disappointed when I saw a bunch of White faces. Although I had a handful of White teachers who I loved, I never quite connected with any of them the way I did with Mrs. Wright. Our relationship was special because she was like me.

I recently shared my struggles growing up with all-White teachers with my friend Kendall, who is a Black female scientist with a PhD in Biomedical Engineering from Cornell University. Kendall told me that she had the same experiences growing up. She seldom had the privilege of having teachers to whom she could relate. However, like me Kendall had also had a handful of Black educators who drastically influenced her academically. She was particularly grateful to her undergraduate chemistry professor, Dr. Ellis.

For Kendall, Dr. Ellis made science relatable in a way that no one had before. Kendall has a head full of naturally curly brown hair that looks as soft as cotton candy. Instead of using generic obscure examples, Dr. Ellis talked to Kendall about why her hair was curly and explained the science behind how chemical relaxers affect naturally curly hair.

I have a lot of Black friends who have never had the experience of having a Black teacher. Many of them spent their lives thinking they hated science or were bad at math, when they may just have had a hard time connecting with their teachers. I'm thankful for teachers like Mrs. Wright and Dr. Ellis who play a role in helping Black kids like myself feel seen, heard, and understood in the classroom.

CHAPTER 17
BLACK GIRL, WHITE SCHOOL

Through my entire academic career I only had one goal, to get into a good college. Both my parents earned their bachelor's degrees from Cornell University, a highly ranked Ivy League school in upstate New York. They instilled in my siblings and me both an appreciation for education and a drive for success.

As a high school student, choosing a college felt like one of the biggest decisions I would ever make. I believed the college I picked would determine the job I was offered, and the job I was offered would determine not only my quality of life but my worth to society. Choosing the wrong school could ruin my life before it even began.

When I was in the tenth grade, I made a list of schools I wanted to attend. Most of the schools on my list, including UVA where I'd eventually end up, were PWIs, or "predominately White institutions." I also considered attending a historically Black college like Spelman or Hampton, otherwise known as HBCUs. I had never been in an all-Black environment before, and the possibility intrigued me. I wondered what it would be like to have Black teachers and lots of Black friends.

My dad's little sister, Auntie Kori, was a Spelman alumnus. Spelman, located in Atlanta, Georgia, was not only a Black school but an all-female school. Auntie Kori loved her experience at Spelman, and strongly encouraged me to attend.

In the end, I decided to go with a PWI. As intriguing as attending a Black school sounded, deep down, I believed that attending a predominantly White institution would lead me to greater success. After all it was White people in America and not Black people who held all the power.

I made the early decision to apply to UVA. It was the highest ranked public university in Virginia and the second ranked public university in the country. With a GPA over 4.0, an exceptionally high SAT score, and a long list of extracurricular activities and leadership positions, I was confident that I had a good chance of being admitted.

When UVA sent me a letter of acceptance in the winter of 2006 I jumped up and down and ran circles around my house. My parents embraced me with tight squeezes and told me how proud they were. All my hard work had paid off. I couldn't wait to tell all my friends that I had been accepted.

When I arrived at school the next day, I learned UVA had also accepted a few of my friends. I was the only Black person from my school who had been accepted, but I was used to being the only Black one. At lunch, we all sat together and talked about how excited we were to start school in the fall. We gossiped about who else had gotten in, who had been wait-listed, and who had been rejected.

Mary got in. Anne got in. Katie did not. Paul Priestley was wait-listed. Katie's and Paul's class rankings weren't quite as high as my own, but they were good students. I felt bad when I thought about how disappointed they must have felt as the rest of us celebrated. We were taught a lot of things in school but learning how to handle rejection was not one of them.

Paul was in my history class later that afternoon. Instead

of awkwardly avoiding eye contact, I decided the mature thing to do would be to offer my condolences about the waitlist. Unlike Katie he still had a shot at getting accepted.

I didn't even have a chance to approach Paul because as soon as he walked into the classroom, he approached me. "You know you only got in because you're Black," he said, loud enough for everyone to hear. He told me that he had been wait-listed and that I had taken his spot. He wondered why I had felt the need to apply to a White college in the first place when there were plenty of Black colleges for me to attend.

My heart raced. Why would Paul think that he deserved to be admitted to UVA over me? Not only were my grades higher than his, but I was far more involved in school extracurricular activities. I was a member of the National Honor Society, the Key Club, and Vice President of the Spanish Honor Society. I ran track. I played basketball. I danced. I was a thespian. I was the star of our high school musical. I even had my own morning show where I read the morning announcements.

I wish I could have stood up to Paul. I wish I could have told him that could go to whatever school I wanted. I wish I could have told him that I had been admitted into UVA not because of my race, but because I was qualified. But instead I said nothing. I was embarrassed. I felt sick to my stomach for the rest of the day. I wondered who else was whispering behind my back about a college acceptance I didn't deserve.

Ironically, Paul was removed from UVA's waitlist and granted admission just a few months later, and as it turned out, I hadn't taken his spot after all. But he never apologized. He never even brought it up again.

CHAPTER 18
THE BIG, WHITE ROOM

The summer after I graduated from law school, my little sister Nia and I went on a mission trip to Nicaragua with a group of seven White people from our church. Our church was a small predominately White Pentecostal church in Haymarket, Virginia. The head pastor, Pastor Brian, was a middle-aged White man with a big personality and a dry sense of humor. He had been my youth pastor since middle school.

I was studying for the Maryland Bar Exam when we left for Nicaragua. My friends and family thought I was crazy for taking on a mission trip while studying for such a demanding exam, but I was determined to both. Serving was important to me. I had always wanted to go on a mission trip, and I didn't know how much free time I'd have once I started working full time. In spite of everyone's concerns, I packed up my books and flashcards and headed to Nicaragua.

We spent two weeks in Nicaragua. While there we helped build a classroom for at risk youth, planted gardens to create sustainable food sources for people in the community, and spent time with the local children. People often say that you benefit more from serving on a mission trip than the people you serve do. As clichéd as it sounds, I found it to be true of my experience on that trip. I left Nicaragua with an abundance of gratefulness in my heart for my friends, my family, and the everyday luxuries, like running water, that so many of us take for granted.

On the way home our group had a two-hour layover in Houston, Texas. Although I was exhausted and couldn't wait to get home, the experience was rewarding. But before we could board, my sister and I were plucked from our group and randomly chosen to have our bags searched at customs. The customs agent who stopped us was a White man with a skinny nose in a uniform that looked two sizes too big for his feather-like frame.

One leader in our group attempted to explain to the customs agent that we were all together, but the agent insisted that my sister and I had to follow him. I asked the agent why my sister and I were the only ones in our group who were being searched. He ignored my question and again instructed my sister and me to follow him. His face was stone cold, and his tone of voice was even colder.

Frustrated, I turned around to assure the White members of our group we'd be okay. I felt embarrassed and ashamed when I saw the look of pity in their eyes. They looked at us like we were abused puppies. Reluctantly, Nia and I followed behind the unfriendly agent.

He led us to a large white room on the outskirts of the airport that was full of Black and Brown people, many of whom could not speak English. The room was a sweatbox, full of loud fans that didn't seem to be doing much of anything. People waited in four separate lines that snaked around the room like a maze.

Although I only spoke remedial Spanish, I understood enough to decipher the many conversations happening around me. I watched one woman sob as she attempted to explain to one of the White, male, English-speaking agents in Spanish that she could not understand him. Another woman cried out that she'd been separated from her children and wanted to know if they were okay. My heart beat fast as I looked around the room at all the distressed faces around me. I wondered if my face looked like theirs.

They sent Nia and me to the end of a long line in the corner of the room. The line moved slowly, only inching forward every few minutes. Our flight was scheduled to board in an hour, and I was afraid we were going to miss it. I wondered if our group was worried about us or if they'd leave us behind in Texas if we didn't make it to the plane in time. With each passing moment my anxiety grew.

After forty-five minutes of standing in line, we made it to the front. A White male customs agent began to ask us questions. His tone was even colder than the customs agent who had pulled us away from our group. This new agent asked me about our trip to Nicaragua, about my family, and about my life back home. He typed notes vigorously on a big black computer as I responded, barely looking in my direction as I answered his questions.

When I told the agent that I was a recent law school graduate studying for the bar exam, he looked up from his computer and squinted curiously in my direction. He grilled me about what school I attended, what I had studied, and what I planned to do when I passed the bar exam. I didn't know what any of his questions had to do with verifying my citizenship, but I answered them all as graciously as my thinning patience allowed.

After questioning me he moved on to my sister Nia. He asked her about her history with drugs and her motivation for leaving the country. Nia was only sixteen and didn't even have her driving license yet. I hated that she was being subjected to questioning without our parents. To protect her from further interrogation, I reminded the agent that our flight was about to board and begged him to let us go. He ignored my request and continued to grill Nia.

When I attempted to jump in to help Nia answer a question, the agent told me to be quiet. He continued to interrogate Nia for fifteen more minutes. Fed up, I told the agent that he had asked her enough questions. I also asked him why everyone in the room had brown skin, and why the White members of our group had been allowed to go. I told him that I felt it was discriminatory and unfair.

Apparently amused by my question the corners of the agent's mouth turned up slightly. He could smile after all. He joked that if I had really graduated from law school like I said I had, then I would understand that unlike standard police officers, he and the other customs agents could be as discriminatory as they pleased. Their job was to protect the border, and that meant stopping people who looked dangerous and suspicious.

Apparently, having brown skin made you public enemy number one. I felt a ball of rage rise within me. My hands instinctively balled up into fists by my side. I told the agent that their practices were unacceptable, and threatened to write a letter of complaint as soon as I got home. He laughed at my empty threat and ensured me that writing a letter would be a waste of my time. As far as he was concerned, he was only doing his job.

I took a deep breath. I wanted to cry and scream, but I knew that would only make things worse. He'd probably have me detained. Moreover, I didn't want to turn into the dangerous person he already believed me to be.

Just when I thought things couldn't get any worse, the agent informed us that he needed to search our bags. Feeling powerless I handed him my bags and instructed Nia to do the same. He searched every corner of my suitcase aggressively, tossing my neatly packed clothing all over the place. My bar exam flash cards, accompanied by my tattered bible, were strewn across the floor.

When he didn't find anything incriminating in my bags he moved on to Nia's bags. He was just as careless with her things as he had been with mine. When he finally finished rummaging through our belongings, he instructed us to bend down and pick them up. So we did. We picked everything up from our dirty underwear to our toothbrushes, stuffing them back into our suitcases as quickly as possible.

"You can't treat us this way, it's not right," I said, attempting to choke back my tears.

Ignoring my comment, the agent told us we were free to go. A knot formed in my stomach as I looked around the room at all the other Black and Brown people being questioned and searched like we had been. I had been so consumed by my own emotions, I almost forgot that hundreds of other people were in the room with us. I wondered how the rest of our White group members were fairing, and if they'd believe me when I told them about our experience in the big, white room.

I had little time to process the experience, because at that point we had less than fifteen minutes to book it across the airport. We made it to the gate just as the woman at the counter announced that boarding was about to begin. My stomach growled as I wiped the sweat from my forehead. I am usually freezing cold on airplanes, but after spending over an hour in a hot sweatbox I couldn't wait to board the air-conditioned plane.

I spotted the rest of our group in line to board the plane. They chatted amongst themselves, smiling, and laughing. One of the church leaders held what looked like a brown bag of leftovers. I realized they had probably sat down for a group lunch at one of the restaurants in the airport. I wondered if anyone had thought to get any food for Nia and me.

"I'm glad you made it!" one of our leaders exclaimed when she noticed Nia and me approaching. "That was really messed up the way they stopped you both, huh?"

Silence.

I looked at their eyes full of both curiosity and pity. No one knew what to say. I wanted to tell them that what happened to us was more than just "messed up." It was both racist and bigoted. I wanted to tell them about the big white room full of fans with long, winding lines of people, all with dark skin. I wanted to tell them about the heartless customs agents and the way our things had been searched and scattered.

But I didn't have the energy to have that conversation. I felt defeated and emotionally drained. I didn't want to relive the experience. I wanted to forget it.

After a few moments of silence, a few of the other group members expressed how glad they were we didn't miss the flight. Nia, who looked a lot more at peace than I felt, told them that there had been only Black and Brown people in the room where the agent took us. Another awkward silence followed. It was clear we were all uncomfortable talking about what had happened.

The conversation quickly transitioned. We chatted about how great our trip had been and other empty niceties. When the man carrying the bag of leftovers put it in his backpack, I realized that no one had thought to grab food for Nia or me. I felt my stomach growl again. We boarded the plane a few minutes later, and never again discussed the incident in the big, white customs interrogation room.

Following the death of George Floyd on May 25, 2020, five years later, the mother of one of the young men on our mission's trip called me. I was surprised to see her name, Nancy, pop up on my phone. I was living in Los Angeles at the time and had not spoken to her or her son in years.

Nancy wanted to talk to me about racism. She was disturbed by the racial division happening in our country, and wanted to know how she, as a White woman, could do her part to make things better. She told me that while having a conversation about racism with her family the other night at the dinner table, her son and daughter-in-law told her about how Nia and I had been singled-out, detained, and searched at the airport on our way home from our mission trip years ago. She couldn't believe something like that would happen in America.

I gave Nancy a detailed description of what happened on our way home from Nicaragua. At that point, I had already processed it with family, friends, and my therapist, so recounting the experience for Nancy was much easier than it would have been years prior. She was horrified and expressed how deeply sorry she was that Nia and I had experienced such appalling treatment.

Nancy and I talked for an hour about other times throughout my life that I experienced discrimination as a Black woman. She listened intently, sporadically offering up her condolences. Though I appreciated Nancy's call, I resented the fact that what had been a traumatic airport experience for me was nothing more than a casual dinner table conversation for Nancy and her family. I still can't step foot in an airport without thinking about the big white room full of distressed Black and Brown faces.

PART 6
BLACK GIRL, NOT MAGIC

When I was in high school, I had an affinity for *Teen Vogue* magazine. Reading *Teen Vogue* made me feel cool. I loved the glossy, brightly colored pages full of fashion and life advice. I used to beg my dad to let me add the trendy magazine to the conveyor belt while waiting in-line at the grocery store. He always said yes.

I rarely saw anyone that looked like me within the pages of *Teen Vogue*. Most of the time, the covers were graced with beautiful, skinny White girls like Taylor Swift, Amanda Seyfried, Blake Lively, Hilary Duff and Mandy Moore. Each month, I scoured the pages for girls who looked like me, looking for validation that my beauty was worth highlighting too. On the rare occasion that they included Black girls, they were often of mixed race with long, shiny hair and European features.

Teen Vogue wasn't the only magazine that left Black girls out of its pages. *Seventeen*, *Cosmopolitan*, and *Elle* also primarily highlighted and catered to White women. The makeup tutorials featured lip colors and foundation shades for White women's skin, and most of the articles were written by White women who seldom considered how their descriptions of their experiences were colored by their privilege.

I don't believe the creators of or contributors to the popular teen magazines of the early 2000s were consciously racist, but the messages they sent were clear. To them, Black girls were not magic. They weren't even worthy of mention.

CHAPTER 19
WHITEOUT

In May of 2010 as a third-year student at the University of Virginia, I competed in my first beauty pageant. A friend of mine asked me to compete in the Beta Sigma Pageant, a campus pageant run by the Sigmas, a Black fraternity on grounds. It sounded like fun, so I happily agreed.

I didn't invite my friends or my family to watch me compete for the title. To me, it didn't feel like a big deal. I grew up watching pageants like Miss America and Miss USA on TV, and I was obsessed with the movie *Miss Congeniality*, but I had never heard of a Miss Beta Sigma. I didn't really prepare for the pageant. I didn't practice my walk or my song for the talent portion. I figured I could wing it and do a decent enough job. I walked away as the first runner up.

When I was twenty-three years old, I competed in my first real pageant. I was a second-year law student at the University of Virginia, and I had just broken up with my boyfriend of five years. Stressed out by a combination of my breakup, my rigorous academic schedule, my student loans which at that point were over $100,000, and a general fear of the future, I was desperate for a way to take my mind off all my problems.

That fall, I received an invitation in the mail from the Miss America Organization to compete for a local pageant. If I won, I'd receive scholarship money for school. It felt like a sign. This was my shot at winning a real pageant title.

My Mom initially laughed when I told her I wanted to compete. She didn't understand why I would subject myself to a panel of judges who would rate my beauty on a scale of one to ten. Many of my friends were similarly baffled. They felt like I should be focused on law school, not parading around a stage in a dress.

The more pushback I received the more determined I was to compete. I watched old YouTube videos of Miss America on repeat, attempting to mimic their smiles and their poses. I practiced walking up and down the narrow-carpeted hallway of my small apartment in a swimsuit and high heels. To prepare for the talent portion, I sang lots of karaoke in my living room. I felt confident and ready to compete.

In January of 2013, I competed in the local Miss Chesterfield pageant. The winner of the pageant would compete for the highly coveted title of Miss Virginia. When I arrived on the day of the pageant, I was much more intimidated than I thought I would be. The other contestants were all much more prepared than I expected.

They toted decorated pageant suitcases, special dress bags for their expensive gowns, bedazzled swimsuits, full length mirrors, and fancy jewelry boxes. Physical trainers, pageant coaches, and hair and makeup artists accompanied many of them. On the other hand, I showed up backstage alone with an old swimsuit and my high school prom dress stuffed into a tattered, black duffel bag.

My family, whom I'd invited to watch me compete for the title, felt just as out of place as I did. Outside of a few gay male pageant coaches, my dad was one of the few men in the crowd. My mom, who rarely took the time to do her hair or her makeup, wore jeans, an old baggy sweater, and glasses. The other mothers wore mascara, pearls, brightly colored dresses, and fine silks. They wanted to be photo-ready just in case their daughters won the crown.

Despite my limited pageant experience, I believed I could win. I felt prepared. I was a pretty good singer thanks to my many years in school chorus classes and church choir, so I knew I would score high marks in the talent portion. I was also confident that I would crush my on-stage question. Law school had prepared me for answering tough questions on the spot.

The moment I stepped on the stage, a wave of excitement pulsed through my body. I loved the crowd, the bright lights, and the cameras. Though my old dress was a bit too short and too tight, its black beads glistened under the lights. I hit every note of my song, and I knocked my on-stage question out of the park. I was on fire, and I knew it.

When the time finally came to announce the winner, I had butterflies in my stomach. I stood on stage in my little black gown along with the other women vying for the crown, waiting to hear my name called. I watched as different women walked to the front of the stage and collected roses as the announcer named the second and first runners-up. I waited for what felt like an eternity for the announcer to name the winner. And then I heard my name.

I had not yet learned the art of how to put on the graceful, surprised face I'd seen on so many other pageant queens. Instead, I jumped up and down like a kid in a candy store, dashing to the front of the stage as quickly as I could manage in my six-inch heels. The crowd burst into applause as the former title holder placed the crown on top of my head. Swarms of arms surrounded me, hugging and pulling me in every direction.

They invited my family on stage to pose for pictures. I can still remember the look of shock on my mom's face. She hadn't expected me to take home the crown.

"I can't believe it," I remember her saying. "I can't believe you did it. You actually did it."

I loved being Miss Chesterfield. As an official Miss America title holder, they gave me a platform to talk about things that mattered to me. I was invited to speak at schools, visit sick patients at hospitals, and ride the float at parades. I talked about how to turn dreams into attainable goals, and the importance of education. When I spoke while wearing my crown and sash, people stopped and listened to what I had to say.

One evening, I was invited to be a guest of honor at an education fundraiser in Richmond, Virginia, along with another beauty queen from Virginia Union University, a historically Black college. She had a beautiful caramel complexion and wore a classy gray suit and a string of pearls around her neck. The event was small, but we had a great time chatting with one another and interacting with guests.

The next day, I called a friend from school to tell her all about that appearance and my new friend from Virginia Union University. I casually mentioned that I was the only *real* beauty queen there that evening. When my friend asked me what I meant by the word "real", I paused.

"I mean, she didn't win a real pageant, she won a Black pageant," I explained.

To me Black pageants weren't credible pageants. The winners of Black pageants didn't compete for a national title on cable television like Miss America's contestants. They weren't invited to the White House to meet the President, or asked to host the MTV awards. They were pretty girls with sashes and crowns, but they weren't real pageant queens.

The Miss America Organization is recognized as one of the first and most prestigious pageant systems in America, and historically is a very White organization. The first Miss America pageant took place in 1921, but for the first thirty years of the competition, Black women weren't even allowed to compete. Finally in September 1983, Vanessa Williams became the first African American to win the title as Miss America 1984.

Vanessa Williams may have been a Black woman, but she was a palatable Black person. She had many of the White European features pedestaled by the pageant community. She was a light-skinned, slender woman with light eyes and straight hair who was well spoken. The message her victory sent to other Black women was that if they hoped to win a crown one day, they too needed to look and sound as White as possible.

CHAPTER 20
THIGHS THAT TOUCH

In November 2013, I competed for the title of Miss Virginia USA as Miss Chesterfield and walked away as a semifinalist. But I wasn't ready to stop competing. I loved it too much. I continued to compete in various White pageant systems over the next few years.

I understood early on that if I wanted to have a successful pageant career, I needed to look and sound as White as possible, just like Vanessa Williams. I couldn't be too Black or too progressive. White pageant coaches encouraged me not to post anything too "woke" on social media or make any statements that were too liberal or politically polarizing. I needed to be relatable and digestible.

I didn't have Vanessa's light skin or green eyes, so I had to find other ways to compete. I learned how to do my makeup in a way that made my Black nose look thinner, and I wore premium, silky-straight hair extensions that looked nothing like the kinky hair that naturally grew out of my head. I even got a spray tan like the White women I competed with to make my brown skin look more bronze than it already was.

When I arrived at my first Palm Beach spray tan appointment, the White woman working the counter looked confused. I was the only Black person in the facility, and my skin was much darker than the darkest shade they offered. I explained that I was a pageant competitor, and I wanted my skin to glow on stage. The woman at the counter placated my request and sprayed me with a translucent, shiny solution. When she finished, it looked like I had taken a bath in baby oil.

I also took nutrition advice from other White contestants. Since physical fitness was a big piece of the score, many of them went to extreme lengths to regulate their body size. One of the women I competed with convinced me that if I wanted to maintain a slender physique, I should snack on baby food instead of food for adults. She explained that baby food was packed with nutrients and half the calories. Against my better judgment, I took her advice and replaced all the cereal in my kitchen cabinet with Gerber Puffs.

In 2014 I won the title of Miss Roanoke USA, and the opportunity to compete for the title of Miss Virginia USA. The Miss USA organization, which began in 1952, was another prestigious American beauty pageant system. Like Miss America, the Miss USA pageant has historically been a predominately White pageant. They did not crown their first Black woman until 1990 when Carole Gist took home the crown.

As part of my Miss Roanoke USA package, I won a free session with a well-known physical trainer in the pageant community named Tom. Tom was a middle-aged White man who had successfully trained several former title holders. I wasn't exactly an Olympic athlete when I started training with Tom, but at 115 pounds and a size two, I was in pretty good shape. During our first training session together, Tom performed a full body assessment.

"You have a great figure, but we're going to have to work hard at getting your butt and your thighs to a good size," he explained.

I knew I needed to do some light toning, but I saw nothing wrong with my figure, especially my butt and thighs.

"Your thighs touch, and that's not ideal," Tom continued. He explained that my butt was too big, and disproportionate to my small legs. He told me that Black women tend to have a lot more junk in the trunk, but that he'd do his best to help me get rid of the excess fast.

Tom's comment sobered me up and got me out of the whitewashed fantasy land I'd been living in. I liked both my thighs and the junk in my trunk. I wasn't about to let some White man tell me how to feel about my body.

When I left my training session that day, I couldn't stop thinking about what he said. He wanted to *fix* me. But it was deeper than that. He specifically wanted to fix the parts of me that he deemed to be too Black. I never told Tom how offensive his comment was, but I did send him an e-mail the following day letting him know that I wouldn't be returning.

Whether it was because of my too-thick thighs, or some other reason, I didn't win the title of Miss Virginia USA that year. However, I did win the title of Miss Congeniality. In other words, the other pageant contestants voted me the most likeable contestant. It wasn't the title I originally wanted, but it was an honor nonetheless. The other White girls liked me. I was officially one of them.

There were lots of things I loved about competing in pageants. I grew in confidence and in my ability to communicate effectively. I met lots of strong, incredible women from across the country. I learned to see my femininity as an asset instead of a liability. However, there was an undeniable dark side to competing.

I now realize that for me, winning a White pageant meant more to me than having a panel of judges tell me that I was smart, talented, and beautiful. It was validation that I had fully assimilated into and been accepted by White America. I had competed against beautiful White women with long blonde hair and blue eyes and won. It was a sign that I was just as good, if not better, than the White women who represented the all-American ideals of beauty and grace.

CHAPTER 21
50 SHADES OF BLACK

    I met Chika in the summer of 2017. We worked together at a fashion and beauty company in West Hollywood. Chika's office was down the hall from mine. She was one of the few Black women at the company.

    Chika had luscious chocolate brown skin and full pink lips. Her natural hair was cut close to her head, which only accentuated her beautiful African facial features. She was well put together, her shoes always equal parts practical and stylish. I loved watching her walk down the hall with her head held high and her laptop in hand.

    Chika had already been working at the company for a year when I started, and she had a reputation for being excellent at everything she did. Intrigued, I offered to take her to lunch. We had a great conversation about our professional goals, our hometowns, and how hard it was to be Black women in White corporate America.

    I told Chika that I loved her short natural hair and asked her what inspired her to cut it. She told me that growing up she resented her natural hair, and like many young Black girls in America she wanted her hair to be straight. However, as she grew older, she learned to embrace her natural texture.

Our conversation about Black hair led to a conversation about colorism in the Black community. Colorism is the evil stepsister of racism. It is defined as discrimination against individuals with a dark skin tone, typically among people of the same ethnic or racial group.

Brown skin girls like Chika and me are all too familiar with colorism. From music videos to corporate America, lighter skinned women are often favored and given preferential treatment in comparison to their darker skinned sisters. Traits attributed to dark skinned women with West African features like wide noses and kinky hair are often deemed undesirable. Even commercials targeting Black communities tend to feature light-skinned women with soft, loose curls instead of brown-skinned women with Afros that stand tall.

Although colorism is a present-day problem, its roots go all the way back to slavery. The mass rape of Black slave women by their White masters gave birth to an abundance of mixed-race children. According to the one-drop rule which stipulated that anyone with even one-drop of Black blood was to be considered Black, the mixed-race children were still considered Black and therefore slaves, but they were treated much better than the other slaves on the plantation.

As brown skinned girls with kinky hair, Chika and I had both grown up feeling inferior to mixed-raced and lighter-skinned Black women. She told me that not long ago, she had given a Ted Talk about colorism in the Black community and the effect it's had on her. Again, I was intrigued.

When I got home that night, I searched for Chika's Ted Talk. To my surprise, her ten-minute talk had amassed over one million views. I immediately pressed play.

In the video Chika explained that in 2015, while getting her MBA at Stanford University, she came across a casting call for the movie *Straight Outta Compton* that openly discriminated against dark-skinned Black women. The movie, a highly anticipated biopic, depicted the rise and fall of the Black rap group N.W.A and its legendary members Eazy-E, Ice Cube, and Dr. Dre. Chika, a huge fan of N.W.A., saw the movie three times.

Straight Outta Compton did well in the Box Office, earning $201.6 million. Like many other people who watched the movie, Chika thoroughly enjoyed it. She loved seeing Black people represented on the big screen and wanted to know more about how the film was made. She scoured the internet looking for everything she could find about the movie. That's when she came across the film's casting call.

Chika was intrigued. She wondered to herself what role she would have auditioned for. She read through the casting call. At the top, she saw a category labeled "A girls." The description for the A girls read:

These are the hottest of the hot. Models. MUST have real hair - no extensions, very classy looking, great bodies.

Chika continued reading through the casting call. Next came the "B girls."

These are fine girls, long natural hair, really nice bodies. Small waists, nice hips. You should be light-skinned. Beyoncé is a prototype here.

Beyoncé. According to the casting directors, even Beyoncé didn't cut it as an A girl. As a dark-skinned girl, the requirement for "light skin" automatically made Chika feel othered. She continued to read about the "C girls."

These are African American girls, medium to light skinned with a weave.

Chika's dark skin not only disqualified her from being a "B

girl", it also disqualified her from being a "C girl." How could a Black movie, starring Black actors and actresses and made for Black audiences, be so blatantly racially discriminatory? Finally, she scrolled to the last category, the "D girls."

These are African American girls. Poor, not in good shape. Medium to dark skin tone. Character types.

After reading the casting call, Chika felt betrayed. *Straight Outta Compton* was a Black movie. It was supposed to be a safe, inclusive space for Black actors and actresses of color. But it wasn't safe. It was triggering.

I looked up the infamous casting call. I wanted to read it for myself. It only took me seconds to find. There it was, in black and white, on a publicly visible web page. Dark skin. The dark skin girls, as they so often are in America, were at the bottom of the casting barrel.

Like Chika, I was deeply disturbed when I read the casting call for *Straight Outta Compton*. According to the descriptions, I was definitely a C or D girl. I wasn't just too Black for White people. I was too Black for Black people.

PART 7
LOVE IS NOT BLIND

    The first time I ever heard a Black boy say he only dated White girls I was in seventh grade. His name was Quincy, and he was the star of the middle school football team. Half the girls in the seventh grade and probably a good portion of the girls in the eighth grade had a crush on him. I was one of the few girls who didn't care for him at all. I thought he was self-absorbed, and I didn't like the way he treated people.
    I didn't know how to feel when I overheard Quincy tell a friend in gym class that he preferred White girls. He said that White girls were more attractive, and easier to deal with. Initially, I was confused. Quincy's brown skin was even darker than mine. His mom had brown skin too. I didn't understand why a Black person with a Black mother wouldn't be interested in dating a Black girl.
    With this new notion that some Black boys preferred girls with White skin, I began to see both the world and myself differently. With the conscious awareness of romantic color preference came a cloud of new insecurities. What was wrong with my brown skin? What made White skin so great? Were

White women prettier than Black women? Were they prettier than me?

While not everyone has color preferences as strong as Quincy's, when it comes to romantic relationship, we must all wrestle with our preferences and why we have them. As much as people like to pretend that they don't see color when it comes to their romantic partners, the truth is that unless you're truly blind, you see color. Like body shapes, we see skin shades and facial features and hair textures. Love, while seldom simple and often intoxicating, is not blind. Love has eyes.

CHAPTER 22
PUPPY LOVE

In kindergarten, I had the biggest crush on a boy named Logan. Logan reminded me a lot of Tommy Pickles from *Rugrats*. He was kind, brave, and very White. He had sandy brown hair, brown freckles, hazel eyes, and a slight dimple. It was love at first sight.

Logan and I were in the same homeroom class at Covenant, the predominately White private Christian school I attended in Charlottesville, Virginia. Our relationship was lighthearted and playful. We both loved apple sauce and Power Rangers. We chased one another at recess and laughed at one another's jokes at lunch.

I also loved Logan's older sister, Jessie. She was in the fifth grade and had long shiny hair the same sandy brown color as Logan's hair. After school I'd stand next to her and Logan at the playground and listen to her talk about what books she was reading, or what she'd learned in school that day. She knew lots of cool things, like the colors of the rainbow and the order of the planets in the solar system.

While I knew that Logan was White, I never took the time

to think about it critically. He never brought up the fact that my skin was darker and my hair was different. He didn't call me "Buckwheat" like some of my other classmates. I always felt like he was being himself when he was with me, and he made me feel like I could be myself too. I had a crush on Logan until the second grade, then I met Dante.

My first memory of seeing Dante was on the playground. He was not in my homeroom class but he was the only other Black kid in the entire grade. That made him easy to spot. He had big brown eyes and Hershey chocolate brown skin. We didn't speak to one another that first day on the playground, but now and then I'd catch a glimpse of him staring in my direction.

After seeing Dante on the playground that day, I felt a rush of guilt about having a crush on Logan. Dante looked more like me. His hair was kinky just like mine. We also shared something that no one else in the second grade shared. We both knew what it was like to be the only Black person in a room.

Growing up, my parents never told me that I should only date boys who looked like me, but I didn't have any reference point for interracial relationships. My parents were both Black and so were all my grandparents. My aunties and uncles were all Black, and those who chose to marry married other Black people.

On the other hand, my White neighbors, my parent's White friends, and my friends' White parents were all married to other White people. My White gymnastics teacher and my White ballet teacher were both married to White men. My disturbingly logical but limited seven-year-old mind quickly came to following life conclusion:

Black people should love Black people, and White people should love White people.

Dante must have felt like he was supposed to like me

too, because soon after his arrival at the Covenant school, we started spending our time at recess together. However, I quickly learned that Dante and I didn't have much in common outside of our shared skin color and the experiences of being different from everyone else. We never played Power Rangers and he didn't laugh at my jokes the way Logan did. But we kept hanging out anyway. We hung out faithfully until my family moved to Georgia the summer after my second-grade year.

Logan was not the only White boy I ever found attractive. Every now and then a White boy would catch my eyes. There was Shawn from summer camp and Billy from church, but I never allowed myself to take any of them seriously. I'd giggle and divert my eyes from theirs when they complemented my pretty brown skin or asked me to go roller skating. I was determined to be with a Black man. I wanted the type of Black love my parents had.

Although we grew up in the same house and were raised by the same parents, my baby brother Johnathan did not experience the same racial cognitive dissonance that I did with interracial relationships. White girls loved my brother and he loved them too. From the time he was a little boy he had lots of little White girls chasing him around the playground. As his body changed from Black boy to Black man, the chasing turned to batted eyelashes and "meet me after school" texts.

Johnathan was also a world class charmer. As far as Black men went, he was the kind of Black boy that White girls felt like they could take home to their mothers. He was an honor roll student, a member of the high school basketball and football teams, and a talented singer. I often rolled my eyes as I watched girls twirl their hair between their fingers as Johnathan played the piano and serenaded them in our family dining room.

I generally liked the girls Johnathan dated. He and I were close, and his girlfriends knew better than to get on my bad side. My interactions with them were usually limited but friendly. We'd smile and wave at one another when we crossed paths and have pleasant conversations when he invited them over for a family dinner.

Although I always picked on Johnathan for only dating White girls, it wasn't until I started processing my own relationships in therapy that I realized how his romantic patterns had affected me. A part of me resented the fact that he preferred to date White girls. As his Black older sister, it was hard not to internalize his preferences as a rejection of Black women. The girls he deemed the most desirable didn't have brown skin and kinky curls like mine. They looked more like the Barbie dolls I idolized as a little girl.

CHAPTER 23
ATTITUDE LIKE MICHELLE

In my late teens and early twenties, I dated a series of Black men with whom I had very little in common other than the color of our skin. Since both my high school and my college were predominately White, there weren't a ton of Black men to choose from. If I wanted a Black boyfriend, I couldn't afford to be too picky.

I started dating my high school bae Marcus when I was in the tenth grade. Marcus and I were like night and day. I wanted to attend an elite college after I graduated, and he didn't want to go to college at all. I was a Christian who attended church and youth groups weekly, and he didn't know whether he believed in God. For the most part I tried my hardest to follow all the rules. I didn't smoke, I didn't drink, and I didn't sneak out at night. Marcus broke the rules every chance he got.

When I was in the twelfth grade, I found out that Marcus had cheated on me with a White girl who sat in front of me in physics. I locked myself in my room for three days and cried until my eyes were puffy. Our relationship ended soon after.

The next fall as a first-year student at the University of Virginia I met my college bae Rafael. He was tall, dark, and handsome, and had the whitest teeth I'd ever seen. He was a football player at the University and had big dreams of playing in the NFL one day. I felt safe with Rafael, but as with my high school bae I quickly learned that we didn't have much in common.

I enjoyed reading novels and going to plays. Rafael liked reading ESPN magazine and hanging out at the bar. We also had different ideas about marriage. He wanted his future wife to stay home and raise his kids like his mother had done. I had no intention of being a stay-at-home mom. Soon after graduating college, I broke up with Rafael. He was heartbroken and I felt terrible.

After a series of flings with other Black men after college and years of telling myself that I would never date anyone other than a Black man, I decided to test the waters with men of other races. First, I dated an Asian man. Then a Latino. Neither of those relationships felt like the right fit either.

Shortly after I moved to Los Angeles, my friend Jessie sent me a text asking how I felt about going on a blind date with a White man named Luke who also lived in Los Angeles. Jessie was a Black woman my age who was married to an older White man. She and I had been close friends since college, and she knew that I had never dated a White man before. Jessie insisted that Luke, who was a friend of her husband's, would be a great match for me.

I've never been a fan of blind dates, but Jessie is not one to take "no" for an answer. If she wanted to, she could sell wool to a lamb. I begrudgingly agreed to meet Luke. I figured if I was going to go out with a White man, it would be better to go out with one who had already been vetted by someone I trusted.

Luke and I met for brunch at a small outdoor restaurant not too far from Hollywood. He arrived at the restaurant before I did. When the hostess walked across the front patio to our table, I was pleased to find an attractive White man with strong masculine facial features and salt and pepper hair.

Luke was about ten years older than I was and had a strong Swedish accent. He told me that he grew up in Sweden and still went back from time to time. Although I spent a good portion of the time trying to decipher what he was trying to say, I didn't mind his accent. Something about knowing that his White ancestors hadn't owned African American slaves made me feel more relaxed.

But that relaxed feeling quickly faded. The more Luke spoke, the less comfortable I became. Five minutes into our date he confidently revealed that he would never date a Jewish woman or a Japanese woman. Apparently, Jewish women had too many religious holidays, and Japanese women were not physically affectionate enough for him. He explained that Black women on the other hand, were not too religious, and not too prude. They were just right.

I winced. Luke talked about Black women like a food option on a menu. A big part of me wanted to challenge his disturbing romantic preferences. How could he say such prejudiced things about Jewish and Japanese people? At the same time, I felt like a hypocrite. Up until then I had never even considered dating a White man. What right did I have to tell Luke who to date when I had my own preferences? Instead of pushing back, I pursed my lips and kept listening.

"My ex was a Black woman," Luke offered, his pink lips turned up into the slightest smile. "I love Black women."

I searched his face for context. Judging by his prior racially insensitive comments and the smirk on his face, my hunch was that he had some type of weird Black girl fetish, but I didn't want to make any assumptions. I asked him to explain what it was specifically that he liked about Black women.

Luke began to list the things he liked about Black women. He was attracted to our strength and our confidence, and he loved how "wild" and sexual we were in bed. Unsure how to respond to this, I stared silently, my eyes wide in disbelief. Just the idea of having sex with Luke sent shivers down my spine. Before I could collect my thoughts, he continued.

"And you ladies have so much attitude."

"Attitude?" I asked calmly. I wanted to school Luke. I wanted to tell him that his racist characterizations were offensive and that women of color were not a monolith to be reduced to a few stereotypes, all the while pointing and circling my finger in his face. But I didn't. I didn't want to prove him right by being a Black woman with an attitude.

"Michelle Obama, for example," Luke continued. "She always has an attitude." Luke rolled his neck, attempting to mimic a Black woman with attitude. He found Michelle's ability to keep Barack Obama in check was attractive.

"Not all Black women are the same," I said as I took a sip of water, attempting to put out the rage burning in my throat.

Luke pushed back. He told me that he had never met a Black woman who wasn't strong, or who didn't have an attitude. He said that was the foundation of what he called our "Black girl magic," and he loved Black girl magic.

The way Luke referred to Black girl magic was off-putting. It felt dirty, like a White master kissing the neck of a Black slave girl covered in sweat from a hard day's work. Even though he recognized the beauty in my Blackness, he couldn't see the invisible battle wounds and burns all over my Black body. The ones that were forged as a kid in the flames of trauma.

I wanted so badly to explain to Luke that my strength, like the strength of so many other Black women, was a byproduct of pain. Black women are strong because we have to be. The ingredients to the magical Black girl potion he was so in awe of were not sugar, spice, and everything nice, but trials, tears, and resilience.

I imagined myself telling Luke to go to hell and causing a scene in the restaurant like a character from a Tyler Perry movie. However, as Black women we must learn how to pick and choose our battles, otherwise we'll spend our entire lives fighting. Fighting White beauty standards, racist government policies, and workplace discrimination. Fighting for inclusion or recognition. Fighting the man. Fighting each other to compete for a spot at the table. Fighting whoever stands in our way.

I had to decide whether Luke was a battle worth fighting. Content for the moment with the hot plate of food in front of me and the hot tea, I could tell my girlfriends later all about my horrible date with the White guy. So I invoked my Fifth Amendment right and remained silent. But Luke just kept talking.

He talked about how White men in America were the true victims. He complained about unnecessary diversity initiatives and lamented about how no one seemed to care about White men anymore. Each comment was more outrageous than the last. As soon as I swallowed the last bite of my salmon omelet, I flagged our waiter for the check.

CHAPTER 24
LESSONS FROM LOVERS

My parents, Sanford and Anastasia, have been happily married for thirty-three years. They still hold hands when they walk down the street, and they still sneak kisses when they think no one is looking. People often compare them to Michelle and Barack Obama, or Claire and Bill Huxtable. They are a power couple with a laundry list of achievements under their belts. To many they are the epitome of Black love.

A few years ago, I asked my mom one day how she and my dad had managed to build such a perfect marriage. I had just started processing through my own relationships in therapy, and I wanted to learn her secrets about how to live "happily ever after." My mom threw her head back and laughed. She said as hard as it might be for me to believe, their marriage had started out as anything but perfect.

My parents started dating as students at Cornell University, an Ivy League school in Ithaca, New York. My dad was an engineering student at the time. He was from Newark, New Jersey, and he was the oldest of four children. He was a child prodigy who graduated from Newark Academy, one of the top high schools in New Jersey, at the age of fifteen. By the time he met my mom at the age of nineteen, he was already in his senior year of college.

My mom was a first-generation Haitian American with butterscotch skin and light brown eyes. Her parents, John and Claudia, were Haitian immigrants who had come to the United States in the 1960s, but she was raised in the Bronx. She was a bookworm who graduated from Bronx Science High School, the number one public high school in New York, with a 4.0 grade average. She was also a singer who had won singing competitions all around the city.

My mom was a freshman in college when she caught my dad's eye at a Delta Sigma Theta event called Jabberwock. Jabberwock was a fundraising variety show, and the proceeds were used to fund scholarships for young women. My mom had been asked to sing a solo number at the variety show. She sang "Via Dolorosa", a melodic song about the resurrection of Jesus Christ.

Mom's stage performance captivated my dad. He loved her sweet voice, the dimple on her left cheek, and her infectious laugh. That evening, he looked her up in the phone book and gave her a call.

My dad asked if he could take my mom out on a date. Initially she turned him down. A devout Christian, she wasn't interested in dating anyone if she didn't feel like she had confirmation from God, or in the words of my mom, a word from the Holy Spirit. My dad graciously accepted her rejection.

After their initial conversation my mom decided to do some research. She started asking people around campus about my dad. She was consistently met with assurances that he was a great guy. People on campus described him as intelligent, dependable, and fun to be around. Whether it was the Holy Spirit or the raving reviews, she decided that she may have been too quick to turn down my dad. The next time she saw him she told him she was ready to go on a date.

On their first date Dad took Mom to the movie theater. When they arrived the ticket line was much longer than they had expected. When Mom said that she was worried they'd miss their movie, Dad smoothly pulled two tickets out of his wallet. He had ordered their tickets in advance.

According to Mom she was immediately smitten. Up until that point in her life she had never been physically intimate with a man. All of that changed when she fell in love with my dad. Just a few short months after beginning to date him, her stomach was the size of watermelon. My dad decided to make an honest woman out of my mom and asked her to marry him. She said yes without reservation.

There was a lot of controversy surrounding my parent's marriage. Like many Caribbean and African immigrants, Mom's parents had preconceived notions about African Americans based on the way they had been represented in the media. They viewed African Americans as lazy, incompetent, and lacking culture. They were not excited to learn their teenage daughter had gone off to college and gotten pregnant by some random African American boy. They knew my mom aspired to become a doctor and they feared that her marrying my dad might get in the way.

Similarly, Dad's parents were not excited about the idea of their beloved eldest son marrying my mom. My dad was well on his way to becoming a lawyer. As far as my grandparents were concerned, my mom was just trying to trap him. They asked him to reconsider his marriage proposal to my mom.

My parents were determined to get married anyway. They were in love, and they weren't going to let anything or anyone get in their way. They didn't have the money for a fancy engagement or a big wedding. Instead they opted to get married at the courthouse. They asked both of their dads to be present as witnesses.

The day they were scheduled to get married, Mom sat with her dad John at the New York City train station and waited for Dad and his dad Joey to arrive. The train was running late, which convinced Mom's dad John that Dad wasn't going to show up. He told Mom that it wasn't too late to change her mind.

Dad's father Joey also tried to talk him out of getting married as they rode the train together to meet Mom and her dad at the courthouse. Like my Grandpa John's efforts, my Grandpa Joey's attempts were fruitless.

My parents were married on December 30, 1988. Over time both their parents came to accept and embrace their relationship. By the time I was born on June 12, 1989, all four of my grandparents were so excited to have a new baby in the family that they cast their fears and concerns aside and came together to welcome me into the world.

Mom and Dad often say that many people spend their lives looking for the perfect love story, not realizing that our job is not to find love but create it. Love is a journey, and everyone's journey looks a little bit different. From them, I leaned never to take anyone I love for granted.

CHAPTER 25
LEFT FIELD LOVE

"You can do this," I said as I downloaded the dating app I told myself I'd never use.

I spoke more words of encouragement over myself as I created my profile. "It's not that big of a deal. Everyone's doing it. If you don't like it, you can just delete it."

Gender? Female.

Religion? Christian. Or spiritual.

Height? 5.5 ft.

Drink? Sometimes.

Smoke? No.

School? The University of Virginia. Better to leave off the "School of Law" part. It might be too intimidating.

Race? Black.

I never understood why dating apps asked what "race" its users were. Wasn't it obvious that I was Black? Anyone looking at my facial features and brown skin would know immediately that I was Black. Then I saw the next question. The app wanted to know what races I preferred to date, and whether my preference was flexible or a deal-breaker.

Immediately, I was discouraged because I knew what that meant. A good portion of the dating pool would never see my profile. They would check the boxes next to White, Latina, Asian, Middle Eastern, Pacific Islander, and American Indian, but not Black.

I knew the statistics. Black women in America were the least desired, and the least likely to get married. According to the 2009 U.S. Census, nearly 40 percent of Black women ages thirty-four to thirty-nine had never been married, compared to 14 percent of their White female peers. A 2014 study on OK Cupid about dating preferences confirmed that this was true even online. Black women received lower ratings than women of any other race, even when rated by Black men.

While I can't fault people for having preferences, I can't help but wonder if those preferences would exist if White beauty standards weren't put on a pedestal in our culture.

Even in the Black community, the whiter a woman looks, the more beautiful she is considered. Black rappers gloat about how they only date light-skinned women, also known as "redbones". Popular Black movies and TV shows like *The Hate U Give* and *Black-ish* routinely cast light-skinned women as their leading ladies. At one point, even historically Black sororities denied admission to women whose skin tone was darker than a paper bag.

The Black men who did check the box next to Black women would likely swipe left only for the redbones, the fair skinned Black girls with good hair, pink lips, and thin noses. They would send them direct messages complimenting their smiles and telling them how much they loved Black women. What they would really mean was they loved Black women with light skin and long hair.

The idea of reducing my life story and my entire character into a multiple-choice quiz that I was statistically programmed to lose felt dehumanizing. Nonetheless, I completed my profile and began to swipe. Left. Right. Left. Right. After twenty-four hours of swiping through hundreds of options, I had only matched with a few men. None of them seemed like viable options. Discouraged by the entire experience, I deleted my profile.

I stopped dating for a while after that. I gave up on not only trying to find Black love but love altogether. I decided instead to focus on myself. I hung out with girlfriends, started a lifestyle blog, took dance classes, and threw myself into my writing. I didn't need a man to validate me, and I wasn't going to wait for one to be happy. And then out of left field came Michael.

I met Michael after a spoken word show in 2015. I was in the crowd, and he was one of the performers on stage. He was Black, but his skin was extremely fair. When we met, I found he was soft-spoken and had a warm smile. His suit was ironed, his shoes were clean, and he smelled like he had just stepped out of the shower.

Michael and I became fast friends. He had grown up in San Diego but had moved to Los Angeles after college. Like me, he was a writer with a passion for social justice. We both had parents who were still married to their first true loves, and we both had little brothers named Johnathan. We were both avid readers and truth seekers.

Michael was charming, sensitive, and a great listener. Although a part of me was attracted to him, I had a hard time relating to him as anything other than a friend. I had no context or experience for how to romantically relate to a heterosexual man who didn't embody the hyper-masculine traits I was used to.

In the South, Black men were encouraged to play football or basketball, or to become a rapper. Baseball and soccer were mildly acceptable alternatives. Anything else made you less of a man. Michael didn't play or watch sports. He was a poet. My friends back home also had no context for a man who preferred words to ball games and were convinced he was gay.

I wasn't exactly Michael's type either. I was a small, dainty southern girl with a lot of opinions and a big personality. I challenged him at every turn. I didn't flirt with him like other girls, and he didn't try to seduce me. Instead, we stayed up all night debating politics and had intellectual conversations about Plato's philosophies.

For a year, our relationship was strictly platonic, but Michael and I spent so much time with one another that eventually the lines between friendship and romance became blurred. One evening at a bar, while in the midst of a heated debate about capitalism, we kissed. The next morning, after having a conversation about how last night had been a mistake, we kissed again.

Friendship is safe and familiar. Romance is dangerous and mysterious. We found ourselves caught somewhere between the two. As a friend, Michael had seen me at my absolute worst, but as a romantic partner, I only wanted him to see me at my best. We struggled over the next few years to find the balance between our friendship and our budding romance.

I also made more money than Michael. It didn't bother me, but it challenged what we had both been taught about the role a man was supposed to play in a relationship. Men were supposed to be the breadwinners and women the help mates. At times Michael struggled with my success, but we always found a way to communicate through the discomfort.

I spent a good amount of time in therapy processing through the relationship between Michael and me. I had waited my whole life for Black love, but our relationship didn't look the way I thought it would. I expected my future husband and I would fall in love at first sight, and that hadn't happened. We were simply two people who wanted to do life together instead of apart.

When I finally let go of trying to put our relationship in a box, the stormy seas began to calm, not just in my mind, but in our interactions. We let go of our respective gender roles and our expectations of one another. I accepted Michael for who he was, and our relationship for what it was. In return, we both felt free to give and receive love.

PART 8
THE CORPORATE CORSET

Growing up in Manassas, Virginia, my family and I were always surrounded by White people. Our mayor was White, our pastor was White, and most of our friends and neighbors were White. We often were the only Black family in the room.

Being the only Black person in the room was exhausting. People asked me questions about my hair, like how often I washed it, and whether it was real. Sometimes people made references to random rap songs I'd never heard of as if I was supposed to know every song written by every Black rapper. I especially grew tired of being asked to be a spokesperson on behalf of all Black people.

As the only Black person in the room, I grew used to navigating in uncomfortable spaces and through awkward conversations. I brushed it off when my neighbors made racially insensitive comments. Whenever a racial issue popped up in the news, the White people in our community turned to my family and me. They asked us for our opinions and to explain the Black point of view. Sometimes, they were receptive. Other times, they grew defensive.

Growing up as the only Black person prepared me for working in a predominately White corporate America. Working in corporate America, I was forced to be productive in the face of inappropriate comments from coworkers and discriminatory policies. Despite my preparation, my experiences were so taxing on my mental health that eventually I made the decision to walk away from corporate America altogether.

CHAPTER 26
WHITE SHOCK

When I was twenty-six years old, I landed a job as a legal assistant at an entertainment agency based in Los Angeles. While in law school, I worked internships at MTV, Fox, and Disney, but I had never worked in such a fast paced and high stress working environment as I found myself in at this new job.

The halls at the agency were busy with the sounds of incessantly ringing phones. People dashed across the office between meetings, barely taking time to look up from their phones. They spoke in industry standard abbreviations that, to the outside ear, sounded like a completely different language.

The agency was overwhelmingly White, and all the top agents were old White men. On my very first day another Black female assistant named Johari told me to make sure not to look any of the agents in the eye. She explained that there was a hierarchy and as Black female assistants we were close to the bottom. Our job was simply to keep our heads down and do what we were told.

I quickly learned that in the entertainment industry everyone must pay their dues. Those dues were different depending on your gender, race, and socioeconomic status. The promise was that if we paid our dues, they would eventually reward us. And if we stayed at the agency we could move up in the ranks. If we left, we'd leave with the best recommendations. Those were the rules, and if you followed them you were bound to be successful. We all wanted to be successful, so we all followed these rules.

While working at the agency I frequently both witnessed and experienced "microaggressions" from White employees. Microaggressions are everyday verbal and nonverbal slights, snubs and insults, whether intentional or unintentional, which communicate negative, derogatory, or even hostile messages based solely upon a person's marginalized group membership. In many cases, these hidden messages demean someone on a personal or group level, or relegate them to inferior status and treatment. They include everything from being left out of social gatherings with White co-workers, to backhanded compliments like, "you're pretty for Black girl." For many Black people working in corporate America, microaggressions are a common occurrence.

One example of such a microaggression is the time I heard my friend Jaden, another Black assistant, tell his boss that he was going to pick up a salmon salad for lunch and that he'd be back soon. Jaden was a former basketball player and had dreams of becoming a sports agent. His boss, Charlie, was an older White man who had worked as an agent for many years.

In a voice loud enough for everyone in the hallway to hear, Charlie asked Jaden why he was ordering a salmon salad instead of fried chicken. I couldn't tell if Charlie was joking or being serious. Jaden laughed uncomfortably and said that he was in more of a salmon mood.

There were seven people in the hallway who heard Charlie's inappropriate fried chicken comment that day, but none of us came to Jaden's defense. At the time I was still new to the company, and I intended to play by the rules. Challenging an agent would be like going outside in a thunderstorm with a metal hanger in hand, a suicide mission.

On another occasion, I overheard one White female agent talking to another White female agent about a group of new Black assistants who had just been hired in the social media department. The agents were unimpressed with the new hires and concluded that they didn't look very intelligent. They chuckled as they made bets about who would be fired first.

I was excited about the new Black hires, and my heart fluttered when I saw them walk in earlier that morning. As a Black girl working in a White space, it's always exciting to see new people who look like you. But my excitement was short-lived. Hearing the agent's comments made me feel sick to my stomach. I wondered if all Black people looked "unintelligent" to the White agents, and if they thought I looked unintelligent too.

It stunned me the first time I experienced a microaggression at work. I was sitting at my desk when a newly hired White female attorney named Helen approached me. Helen was only a few years older than me and sat in a large office across the hall from my small cubicle. I had just hung up the phone with opposing counsel and Helen had overheard our entire conversation.

"Wow, you really know what you're doing," she said as she stood in front of my desk. I smiled, unsure of how to respond. Helen smiled back, and then proceeded to ask me where I went to law school. When I told Helen that I graduated from the University of Virginia School of Law, her jaw dropped.

"You sound surprised," I said, annoyed by Helen's reaction. Helen said she knew that she shouldn't be surprised, but she was. She couldn't believe that I graduated from a higher ranked law school than she herself did.

I looked up at Helen with my eyebrows squinched in disbelief, but I wasn't really surprised that Helen had been taken aback by my academic record because at that point I was used to White people assuming they were smarter than I was. It happened when I went to the dentist, to the grocery store, and to the nail salon. However, I was taken aback that Helen had vocalized how surprised she was.

Usually when White people were surprised by my accomplishments or made assumptions about my education or intelligence level, they tried to hide it. Sometimes, they turned red with embarrassment. Other times, they quickly tried to change the subject. But not Helen. Helen made no attempt to hide her shock.

Helen admitted that I had suddenly become much more interesting to her. She asked me questions about my upbringing and my family. She asked about my career goals, and about my Hollywood apartment. Initially, I was annoyed by Helen's fascination with my life, but as I listened to her talk about her own life my perspective changed.

Helen grew up in a wealthy part of Los Angeles and attended a fancy prep school with a bunch of other rich White kids. She had interacted with Black people before, but she didn't have any real Black friends. Everything about me, from my hair to the way I spent my free time, was shiny and new to Helen. After chatting for thirty minutes at my desk, Helen asked me if I wanted to go to lunch. I accepted her invitation.

Over time, Helen and I grew to be friends. Although we had been raised in different worlds on different sides of the country, we had a lot in common. We were both curious and ambitious. We both loved dogs, good food, and Lionel Richie. She was a great listener and she remembered even the most incidental details about my life. One time she even brought me brown bagel chips because she remembered they were my favorite snack in the Chex Mix bag.

But not all my interactions ended as kindly as my interactions with Helen. I was sitting eating Chipotle at my desk one day when I saw a big white hand reach into the bag of tortilla chips sitting next to me. When I looked up, I saw that the hand belonged to my friend Jaden's boss, Charlie.

Charlie knew I was friends with his assistant, Jaden, but we had never had an actual conversation before. Every now and then I saw him in the hallway, but I always made sure to divert my eyes before we made eye contact. After all he was an agent, and I was just an assistant.

"What's up girlfriend?" he asked as he rolled his neck in a circular motion. I had never heard Charlie call anyone a "girlfriend" before. When he was finished chewing, he reached down and grabbed another large handful.

I froze. I felt my body temperature rise and my heart pound. I sat in silence as he chewed. When he finished eating his second handful, he walked away.

I was furious. I felt violated. Charlie took something that belonged to me without my consent. He made a lot of money, and he could afford to buy his own chips. But he didn't take my chips because he was too poor to buy some for himself. He took my chips without asking because he could.

CHAPTER 27
GREAT EXPECTATIONS

A few years after graduating from law school I attended a three-day continuing legal education conference in Austin, Texas. The conference was held in a massive conference hall downtown.

I had never been to a legal conference before and had no idea what to expect. According to the conference schedule I had received a few weeks prior, each day of the conference was jam-packed with classes, lunches, panels, and networking events spread across the conference hall. In anticipation of the long days, I had packed jeans, sneakers, a few blouses, and a comfortable gray cotton dress that stopped just above my knees.

On the first day of the conference, hundreds of lawyers swarmed the conference hall searching for sign-up sheets and break-out sessions. I showed up in my short gray cotton dress and a pair of black sneakers. I wore my hair in long box braids pulled back into a half ponytail and donned a small black book bag on my back. On the other hand, most of the other lawyers were dressed in nice suits and dress shoes and carried fancy leather laptop bags.

    I felt like a stripper in a Baptist church. Not only was I underdressed compared to the other lawyers, but I was much younger. I was also one of the few Black people at the conference. Many of the older women stared at me intently, and a few of them whispered to each other as I walked by.

    At the end of that first day, I was standing in the middle of a long hallway looking at the schedule for the following day when an older Black woman walked up to me and introduced herself. Her skin was smooth and dark. She had a big smile on her face, and she looked like she was in her mid-sixties. I smiled back at her and introduced myself. I was happy to see another brown face. I had only seen one other Black person that day, and that man had looked like he was older than my grandparents.

    The woman asked me how long I'd been practicing law and if I'd ever been to a legal conference before. I told her that I had graduated from UVA Law School just a few years ago and that I had never been to a conference like this. She said she was happy to see someone my age taking my career seriously. I thanked her for what I interpreted to be a compliment.

    "You are so brave for wearing that nose ring here," she added. I reached up and felt the small gold hoop hanging from my left nostril. I hadn't taken it out since I had my nose pierced the year prior, and I had never even considered removing it for the conference.

    My nose ring felt like a piece of me. I informed the woman that I never took my nose ring out, and that I didn't consider leaving it in for the conference to be an act of bravery. I was just being myself.

    "Being yourself in corporate America is brave," she said. She told me about how she had always wanted a nose ring but could never muster up to the courage to get one. She worked in a conservative office where she was the only Black attorney. The other attorneys even asked questions when she changed up her hair style. One time she wore a head wrap to work and her boss asked her to take it off. She couldn't imagine how they would have responded if she had come to work wearing a nose ring.

Listening to her talk made me feel sad for her. I imagined her growing up during an earlier time where simply being a Black woman in corporate America had been regarded as intolerable for some. I knew what it was like to be the only Black person in the room, but I at least had the benefit of being part of an increasingly tolerant workforce.

Most of the companies I had worked for were full of millennials like me. People came to work with tattoos, blue hair, and graphic t-shirts from their favorite bands. Some men wore earrings, and some women rocked buzz cuts. As long as it wasn't offensive, it was allowed.

I wondered what the woman in the hall would look like if she were free. I wondered what she might wear or how she would style her hair. Maybe she'd have a tattoo or a cartilage piercing. Maybe she'd wear bright gold eyeshadow and have long, seductive eyelashes. Or maybe she'd wear an assortment of precious jewels, flashy rings, and gold bangles.

We talked for a while about our respective jobs and our experiences at the conference. She told me which lectures from the previous year she found helpful, and which speakers were so boring she had almost fallen asleep. She also gave me a few restaurant recommendations for dinner and she suggested a great coffee shop to visit in the morning. I took notes on my iPhone while she talked.

At the end of our conversation the woman, who was still admiring my nose ring, asked if she could take a picture of me. Her question caught me off guard. She explained that she wanted to send it to her husband to show him how brave I was. She seemed earnest, and to my surprise, borderline inspired. I smiled and agreed to let her take my picture. She took a step back, snapped a few photos on her flip phone and then shoved it back into her big black purse.

    I thought a lot about our conversation when I got back to the hotel that evening. Maybe the woman in the hall was right. Maybe being myself in corporate America was an act of bravery. I played with my nose ring as I lay in bed. I made a vow to myself that night that I would never work at any place that didn't allow me to show up as myself. My true, authentic self.

CHAPTER 28
DIVERSITY IS A LIFESTYLE

After a year and a half of working at the talent agency, I was hired as Business and Legal Affairs Counsel at a small beauty company in Los Angeles, California. My boss was a White gay man from New York who wasn't too much older than I was. We both loved musical theater, Legally Blonde, and Oprah. When he complimented my bright green jumpsuit in my interview, I knew we were meant to work together.

There were things about working for the company that I loved. The company had been founded by millennials and offered great workplace benefits. We had unlimited vacation, catered lunches on Fridays, and kombucha on tap. We were also allowed to bring dogs to work. My first week of work I watched a baby yorkie pee in the corner of the room in the middle of a meeting. No one got up to clean it up.

At times working at my new company felt like being in a sorority because 90 percent of the employees were young White women. Most of them looked like Forever 21 influencers. They were the kinds of girls who won prom queen titles and sat at the popular table at lunch in high school. We spent the first thirty minutes of our meetings talking about *The Bachelor* or the latest Kardashian scandal.

Although my co-workers were friendly, I constantly felt like I had to try to correct and educate them when it came to issues of race. My coworkers turned to me with questions whenever we sold products marketed to Black women. I tested lipstick shades, hair bonnets, and conditioners for the merchandise department. I explained Black buying trends to the marketing team, and I told the brand partnership team which Black female influencers they should pursue.

At the time, the merchandising department was trying to sell haircare products to Black women, but they didn't know anything about Black hair. They tried to sell a gel for curly hair in a commercial using a Black model wearing a long, straight hair weave. I had to explain to them that a Black girl wearing a straight weave would never use a gel like that to style her hair.

One time I sat in a meeting where a White female co-worker asked why she couldn't say the "n word." Everyone got quiet. I was the only Black person in the room, so I took it upon myself to respond. I explained to her the painful, racist history associated with the word, and how hearing a White person use the word was traumatic for a lot of Black people.

"It's just a word," she said matter-of-factly. She apparently hated the idea that there was a word she was not allowed to say. She also seemed to believe that as an American, it was her right to use whatever words she pleased. Realizing that nothing I had to say was going to change her mind, I changed my approach. I asked her why she wanted to say the "n word" so badly. Her cheeks turned red at my question, but she didn't have anything to say in response.

Over time I became resentful of having to be the spokesperson for my entire race. I sometimes found myself checking out during meetings. The energy I once had to inform and educate my peers about race-related issues began to fade. I had been hired as an attorney, but I had become a consultant for all things Black.

At a company all-hands meeting three years into my employment there, one of our CEOs introduced us to Kevin, a new director in the HR department. Kevin was an Asian male in his mid-forties, and he had worked for lots of impressive companies with big names. He was tasked with putting together a set of company values for our company. We didn't have any company values before his arrival, but our CEO felt like it was finally time for us to define who were as a company.

The CEO shared with all of us a long list of potential values. The list would be distributed to all of us once it was finalized. I noticed that "diversity" was missing from the list, but I wasn't surprised. Our CEOs were both White men. They probably hadn't even considered adding diversity to the list.

That afternoon I emailed Kevin. I welcomed him to the company and told him that I'd love to be a part of helping to name and narrow down our company values. Kevin quickly responded that he'd love to set up a time to meet.

I met with Kevin in my office a few days later. During our meeting, I told him that I thought it would be a great idea to include diversity as a company value. I explained that our company was growing but I believed we lacked the diversity necessary to move successfully into the future. Black and Latina women represented a large portion of our market, but the White women at our company didn't have the cultural competency required to market to them effectively.

I told Kevin about the White girl who didn't understand why she couldn't use the "n word." I told him that I had been advising all the teams and departments on issues related to race, even though it wasn't part of my job description. I wasn't being paid any extra money for my advice even though other companies paid thousands of dollars for the type of consumer insights I provided.

Kevin nodded his head, listening intently as I spoke. As one of the few other minorities at the company I expected him to understand. There weren't many Asians at our company either. At the very least, Kevin knew what it was like to be the only one like him in a room.

After I finished speaking, Kevin thanked me for sharing. He explained that while he believed diversity was important, it was not going to be a company value. The leadership team had considered including diversity, but they decided they wanted to promote less political company values like kindness and teamwork instead.

I looked at Kevin in disbelief. I did not expect him to shut down my suggestion to include diversity as a company value so quickly. I acknowledged that while kindness and teamwork were important, diversity was not a political matter. I explained that as a company that was increasingly targeting Black and Brown customers, we should make a conscious effort to hire more Black and Brown people. We would all benefit from having people at the table with different backgrounds and perspectives.

Kevin was unconvinced. The leadership team had already made up their mind. He said it was good to know that I was passionate about diversity, and that if the company ever decided to focus on diversity in the future, he'd be sure to include me in the conversation.

In that meeting Kevin confirmed what I already felt in my soul, that diversity was not a priority for the company. I realized that as long as I continued to work there my own well-being and state of mind would not be a priority either.

What the director failed to realize is that diversity is not just a value or an initiative to be picked up and put down like a stack of paper. Diversity is a lifestyle. His inability to see the irony in wanting to sell products to Black customers without making a commitment to diversity was indicative of the company's cluelessness.

    Shortly after my conversation with Kevin I informed my boss that I was leaving the company. After five years of working in corporate America, I was exhausted and burned out by the corporate work environment and the constant insensitivity to issues of race and culture. I needed to take off the corporate corset that was threatening to suffocate me and find something more rewarding to do with my time.

PART 9
WHITE JESUS

    I remember exactly where I was when Beyoncé released her hit Netflix musical film and visual album *Black is King*. I was sitting on my living room coach wearing gray sweatpants and a tattered white t-shirt drinking a glass of Riesling. After quarantining in the house for months thanks to the Covid-19 shutdown, I was excited to have something new to take my mind off the arduous state of the world.

    Within minutes, I fell in love. I fell in love with the music, the breathtaking set design, the costumes, and the storytelling. I was enamored most of all by the unapologetic ethnic splendor. The media often depicts Black people as poor, broken, criminalized, and powerless. It wasn't often that I saw Black people presented in such a powerful way. Fireworks exploded inside me as I watched all the different shades of brown skin dressed in elegant, African inspired garments sing, rap, dance, play, emote, express, and most astonishingly, reign.

    Feeling encouraged, I took to social media to share how excited I was about Beyoncé's new visual album. I shared how capable and powerful the film made me feel as a Black woman.

A few of my friends shared my sentiments and expressed how empowered they also felt while watching the film. However, one of my friends was less than impressed.

She was offended by the title of the film, *Black is King*, because she believed Jesus was the only one who should be referred to as "King." I explained that the film was simply a Black-centered reimagining of Disney's *The Lion King*, but it didn't change her opinion. She was also bothered by what she deemed Beyoncé's irresponsible use of the word "power." In her opinion, it was sinful for Beyoncé to present herself and other Black people as having unlimited power. She likened it to witchcraft or sorcery.

Although I strongly disagreed with my friend's staunch evangelical perspective, having grown up in a White Pentecostal church I understood why she felt the way she did. For a long time, the concept of believing in myself felt sinful. The only thing I was taught to believe in was the redeeming power of Jesus. There was no need talk about whether or not I believed in myself. As long as I obeyed God's word and fled from sin, if he deemed me worthy, God would give me the desires of my heart.

I later realized in therapy that my religious beliefs were the foundation of many of my limiting beliefs. For years my faith led me to see myself as powerless. I saw God as a big scary figure who had complete control over my life. My only job was to make God happy by doing whatever he asked of me, which in most cases was whatever my White male pastors asked of me.

It was not until I let go of this oppressive conception of faith that I was able to see myself as the powerful woman God created me to be. The conversations I have with God now sound much different than they used to. They are not riddled with shame, but with love, gratitude, and a divine recognition of my own power. I no longer see myself as a powerless being, but as co-creator of my destiny.

CHAPTER 29
NOT MY JESUS

    Like many young Black millennials, I grew up going to church with my family every Sunday. My most formative years were spent at a large Pentecostal church in Manassas, Virginia. Besides Sunday morning service, I also attended Sunday school early mornings before service, and young adult service every Wednesday night.

    Our church was overwhelmingly White with just a handful of minorities. True to form, my family was one of the few Black families who attended consistently. Since there weren't many other Black people in the congregation, we stood out amongst the crowd. Most people knew my dad, mom, brother, sister, and me by name. I couldn't sneeze without it getting back to my parents.

    Dramatic stage lights, smoke machines, and full rock bands who played behind small, fashionably dressed worship teams defined White church culture in the early 2000s. The trendiest ones were akin to pop stars. They ditched old school hand-held microphones for Britney Spears style headsets and worked the stage like they were Madison Square Garden headliners.

My church was no exception. The young adult worship team on Wednesday nights dressed in name-brand jeans, graphic t-shirts, and brimmed felt hats. The petite red head woman who led them was a skilled vocalist and an impressive guitar player. She reminded me of a contemporary Christian version of Miley Cyrus.

Every week, the words to the same handful of worship songs appeared on a projector screen behind the worship team as the audience lifted their hands in the air and sang along in harmony. We sang uplifting songs like "Trading My Sorrows" from Darrell Evans's 1998 *Freedom* album:

We say
Yes Lord yes Lord yes yes Lord
Yes Lord yes Lord yes yes Lord
Yes Lord yes Lord yes yes Lord
Amen!

People ran to the front of the stage and jumped up and down to the music like fans at Woodstock. They shouted to the Lord and lifted their hands in the air in worship. I often thought that to people on the outskirts of religion, the entire experience would probably seem cult-like.

After approximately twenty minutes of worship, our youth pastor, a White middle-aged man named Martin, took over the stage and began preaching the good news of Jesus Christ. He warned us against the dangers of the sinful outside world. He told us that listening to any music besides Christian music would lead us into sin and having friends who weren't born again Christians would cause us to stray from God.

We never talked about the insidiousness of racism, injustice, or poverty that existed in our community outside the four walls of our church. Instead, our youth pastor spent a considerable amount of time warning us about the evils of sex and sex's dangerous first cousin fornication. Sex outside of marriage, oral sex, and gay sex, were surefire ways to earn a first-class ticket to hell.

I was taught that as a young woman, my sexual purity was my crowning glory. No respectable man would want to marry a woman who had been deflowered. It was my job to dress as modestly and act as appropriately as possible to keep my fellow brothers in Christ from lusting over me.

Although no one ever explicitly said it, there was also an unspoken understanding that Jesus was a White man. In pictures, paintings, and films shown at church, he was depicted as looking eerily like comedian Russell Brand. He always had long brown wavy hair, European facial features, and a thick manly beard. Dressed in a white robe and open sandals, White Jesus would have fit in with White American hippies in the 1960s.

Jesus wasn't the only biblical figure presented as White. As far as the church was concerned, there were no Black or Brown characters in the bible. Joseph and the Virgin Mary were White, David was White, Esther was White, King Solomon was White, and the twelve apostles were all White. Even the Egyptians and the angels were depicted as White characters.

At first, I kind of liked White Jesus. He seemed happy and friendly, like Barney or Santa Clause. If you were especially good he'd even grant a few of your wish-like prayers. I also liked being part of a church where I was made to feel like I belonged. Although no one looked like me, I was constantly assured that we were all brothers and sisters in Christ's view. That meant we were family.

The sense of belonging I originally felt when we joined the church lessened over time. I didn't know why, but a voice in the back of my mind kept whispering that something wasn't right. White Jesus was not shaking out to be the loving and inclusive father figure I was promised. According to the pastor, he despised welfare, immigration, affirmative action, and every other government program that aided people in need.

According to the pastor, White Jesus also had a confusing stance on gun control. He believed everyone had a right to own guns, but for some reason, he saw guns in the hands of Black and Brown men as a threat. He was forgiving and merciful when young White teenagers made reckless mistakes, but he was full of vengeance when Black kids made bad decisions.

White Jesus also looked down on Muslims, Buddhists, women in leadership, anyone who identified as part of the LGBTQIA+ community, or anyone born in a country other than the United States. Apparently, Americans held a special place in his heart. We were his favorite nation, and it was us, and not any other nation, that deserved his blessings.

One Sunday after church, my friend Joy and I had an interesting conversation about Mexican immigrants at the border. Joy had pale skin, thick curly hair, and a face full of freckles. She was my pastor's daughter and the epitome of a good Christian girl. She was soft-spoken, polite, and modest in the way she dressed. Her ability to maintain such a squeaky-clean image fascinated me. I often wondered if she ever dreamed of rebelling in protest, or if she had any skeletons hiding behind her back. If she did, she hid them well.

Joy's dad had mentioned in the sermon that afternoon that our country was in danger of being destroyed by illegal immigrants. His comment bothered me. I didn't understand why he saw people looking to give their families a better life as threats instead of people in need.

I asked Joy why her dad was so opposed to Mexicans crossing the border. She tilted her head in thought for a moment before she asked me what I would do if I found a homeless man living in the basement of my house.

Her question caught me off guard. I told Joy that my first instinct would be to call the police, but if the homeless man didn't seem dangerous, I'd probably just ask him to leave. "Exactly," she said. I didn't understand.

Joy explained that just like a homeless man living in someone's basement, illegal immigrants had no right to live on land that didn't belong to them. I told her that her analogy, though logical on the surface, was flawed. The land we called America technically did not belong to us, either. It was stolen from Natives who were misled, killed, and displaced. Black slaves then cultivated and harvested it for hundreds of years.

While Black and Brown people who left their countries for new lands were looked down upon, White people who left their countries were called explorers or conquerors. The way I saw it, nothing separated the pilgrims fleeing England years ago from the Mexican immigrants currently crossing our borders other than the color of their skin. If we wanted to get technical, White people were immigrants too.

Joy looked puzzled as I spoke, as if the information was being presented to her for the first time. She told me she had never thought about it that way before. Her dad had never talked to her about the complexities of ownership or the role that race played in how we thought about immigration.

It became clearer to me after my conversation with Joy that I needed to explore what faith looked like outside the four walls of my church. I wanted to know who God was outside the narrow parameters of White evangelicalism, and that was not something a White evangelical pastor could teach me. Initially, I was afraid to question what I had been taught in fear that White Jesus would send me to hell, but over time that fear grew smaller. I was in search of truth, and I was willing to risk everything to uncover it.

CHAPTER 30
THE PRISON OF BELIEF

Following the murders of Ahmaud Arbery, Breonna Taylor, and George Floyd in 2020, I watched an online interview between White Christian leader Christine Caine, and Black minister and mental health expert Dr. Anita Phillips. The conversation centered on the intersection of race and Christianity. A friend of mine suggested I watch the interview between Christine and Dr. Phillips. She believed it would help me process through the complex feelings I had towards the church.

At the time, I had a lot of animosity built up towards the church. While Black communities privately and publicly mourned the untimely deaths of Ahmaud Arbery, Breonna Taylor, and George Floyd, many White churches, said nothing. They continued business as usual, telling the same bible stories they told week after week. It devastated me that so many churches who professed to care about all people remained silent in the face of so much loss and pain in the Black community.

My animosity towards the church poked holes in my faith in God. Streams of doubt leaked from every which way.

I questioned whether God was truly good, and whether he existed at all. I doubted that one conversation would restore my faith in anything, but I agreed to watch the hour and a half long exchange between Christine and Dr. Phillips. Worst-case scenario, it would just be another clichéd Christian conversation about the redeeming love of White Jesus.

In the interview, Dr. Phillips talked about how our racial and cultural backgrounds influence our worldviews, including the way we experience God. She explained how our cultural worldviews influence our religious beliefs and practices. We often think we're debating religious theology when what we're really debating are cultural differences. For example, she explained that the central role the Virgin Mary plays in Latin and Italian Catholicism is indicative of the dominant role of the mother in traditional Latin and Italian families. Similarly, traditional African American Christianity often reflects African movement, African songs, and African sounds.

The culturally manufactured fog in my mind that clouded how I saw God lifted as I listened to Dr. Phillips speak. Hearing her explain how our world views affect the way we see God provided context for the disconnect I had been feeling from the church. I spent the next few weeks critically examining who I believed God was separated from White American influence. I spent a lot of time praying, reading my bible, and consulting other historical texts.

I was reading my bible one day when I came across an interesting passage about Jesus's early childhood in the book of Matthew. It read:

> *Get up, take the child and his mother and escape to Egypt. Stay there until I tell you, for Herod is going to search for the child to kill him. So he got up, took the child and his mother during the night and left for Egypt, where he stayed until the death of Herod.*

I had heard White pastors preach from the book of Matthew countless times as a kid, but not once had anyone mentioned that Jesus spent some of his most formative years in Africa. Jesus had lived amongst Black people and blended in so well that even a King could not find him. Maybe Jesus wasn't a White man after all.

Not only was Jesus probably ethnic looking enough to hide out in Egypt amongst the people, but he was also an immigrant. He crossed the border and left his home country in search of a better life. This Jesus sounded nothing like the judgmental White Jesus who I was taught hated immigration. American Christianity was not an objective source for truth as I was taught, but a subjective interpretation of faith laced in political agendas. The Christianity I was exposed to growing up had cultural notions of racism, sexism, capitalism, and nationalism woven into its fabric. If I wanted to get to know the heart of God, I had to unravel the threads to figure out what was God, and what wasn't.

Inspired, I took to social media to share my revelation. I lamented that American Christianity was so based in White American-centered propaganda that any criticism of America was often interpreted by the church as an attack on religion. Americans killed, enslaved, and oppressed people of color for centuries in the name of Manifest Destiny, an idea originating in the 1800s that America was destined by God to expand its dominion across the North American continent, but anyone who criticized America's history, or its correlating systems of oppression, became an enemy of the church.

A young White male who I'd never met before responded to my post critiquing my criticism of America. The young man agreed that White American Christianity played a role in the displacing and enslaving of people of color. He argued, however, that it was God's will that America become a great colonial nation, no matter the cost. For him, the slaughter and displacement of Native Americans and enslavement of Africans were unfortunate but necessary consequences of America's pre-ordained world domination.

It stunned me as I parsed through his lengthy response. It was clear that he and I did not share the same underlying belief about who God was. I had expected people to push back against the idea that Christianity played a role in the oppression of people of color, but I hadn't expected anyone to suggest that the oppression was actually God's will.

Discovering who I believed God was set me free from the beliefs that held me captive for so many years. I no longer looked to White male pastors or any other spiritual leaders to spoon feed me their own ideas about who God was and what he wanted for my life. Instead, I learned to listen to the voice inside me, the one that had been there all along.

CHAPTER 31
MODESTY IS A CODE WORD FOR CONTROL

It's no secret that in America, Christianity has been used as a tool to oppress Black people. Many Christian slave masters reasoned that slavery would help them bring faith and order to the savage-like Africans they had captured. By this reasoning, slavery was not a human rights violation but a vehicle for discipleship.

Although most slaves were not allowed to read, some slaves were given a special redacted version of the bible. This "slave bible", which is now on display now at the Museum of the Bible in Washington, D.C., excluded any verses or stories that might inspire revolution or civil disobedience. The text of the slave bible did not include any stories about how Moses led the Israelites to freedom. Passages emphasizing equality between all people were also conveniently removed from the text.

Unfortunately, Black people are not the only ones who Christians have oppressed using the bible. They've also used the bible to oppress poor people, LGBTQIA+ people, people with physical and mental disabilities, people with different religious beliefs, and of course, people with vaginas. Like having Black skin, having a vagina relegated you to a lesser position in society.

Growing up, my pastors taught me that if I truly wished to please God, I needed to become a *Proverbs 31 woman*. A Proverbs 31 woman had a loving husband and doting children. She worked tirelessly to care for her family and her servants. She was a good cook, a seamstress, a philanthropist, and on the side a businesswoman. She rarely slept and never did anything for herself. Her sole purpose in life was to meet the needs of others.

Before I could become a Proverbs 31 woman, I had to find a husband. If I wanted a husband, my pastor taught that there was a strict list of rules I needed to follow. I needed to be quiet and agreeable. I couldn't be too flashy, too prideful, or too ambitious. Above all else I needed to be modest.

In the context of the church, modesty was an outward expression of inner purity. We were forbidden from wearing anything that might make our brothers in Christ lust after us. That meant covering your cleavage, wearing skirts past your knees, and choosing loose fitting appeal. Being modest meant being sexually chaste until you were married. No man of God would dare marry a woman who wasn't a virgin.

Despite growing up in church, I never fully bought into the idea that God was a prude who wanted me to be a glorified, self-sacrificing nun with no ambitions of my own. In fact, I flat out rejected it. To the dismay of my pastors, I wore tube tops, bikinis, tight dresses, and Daisy Dukes. I challenged authority, I spoke up for what I believed in, and I assumed positions of leadership at every opportunity I got.

I lost my virginity at sixteen years old to my high school boyfriend. I didn't feel dirty or guilty like the pastor said I should. Instead, I felt liberated. However, I did feel guilty for *not* feeling guilty. I wondered if there was something wrong with my internal moral compass.

I didn't tell my friends at church when I lost my virginity. In fact, I didn't tell anyone. I didn't want to be judged or labeled with a scarlet letter. Looking back, I wish that I had processed my sexuality with my parents, but I was afraid that talking about it would make it more real. If I kept it to myself, maybe God would just his close eyes and pretend it never happened.

I tried again and again to be celibate. Every time a pastor preached a message about modesty I felt dirty. I interpreted this dirty feeling as a spiritual conviction. Each time I made a commitment to myself that I'd stop having sex.

I tried to make my boyfriends commit to celibacy, too. Whenever we felt the urge to have sex, we prayed. After we finished having sex anyway, we prayed again and vowed to do better the next time.

I was having a conversation with my therapist Carrie one evening when she asked me about my sex life. I was dating Michael at the time and we were in a good place. We were growing, chasing our dreams, and supporting one another in the process. We weren't exactly celibate, but we were trying. I was always trying.

I told Carrie that I was trying my best to be celibate because I wanted God's best for my life. She then asked me what God's best for my life was. I didn't know how to respond. I knew what I was supposed to say, a loving husband, doting children, a tireless list of never-ending chores, but I had never really stopped to think about what I *actually* wanted.

I realized when I got home that evening that I was already living God's best for my life. I had a wonderful family, an incredibly supportive partner, and a job that I loved. God wasn't withholding good things from me because I was having sex with someone I loved, someone who loved me. God was with me, in my heart, in my life, and in the bedroom.

A few weeks later, I received a direct message from my pastor on Instagram. It was almost 2 a.m. and he wanted to know whether Michael and I were being celibate. I knew that in his mind, he felt like he was doing me a favor by holding me accountable, but his question made me feel uncomfortable. It felt like a complete invasion of my privacy.

Had my pastor asked me that question a few months earlier, I would have lied, but after processing my sexuality in therapy, I didn't feel like I had anything to hide. I told my pastor that my relationship with Michael was between me and God. He didn't like that answer. I tried to explain to him that we were happy in our relationship, but he didn't like that either.

He told me that I was in denial. He rejected the notion that I knew what made me happy, or what was best for me. I was a woman in love, and a woman in love was not to be trusted. He told me that God had more intended for my life. When I asked him what "more" was, he couldn't tell me.

By the end of our conversation, I was so mad that I was shaking. I didn't know whether I wanted to scream or cry. I realized in that moment that what made me feel dirty was not actually having sex *with* men, but being told for years what to do with my body *by* men. I was not an object to be controlled, but a living, breathing person with my own mind. My own desires. My own body.

PART 10
BODY WARS

In a therapy session with Carrie one evening, I mentioned that I noticed social media influencers with thick thighs, stretch marks, and a little extra belly fat were often characterized here in America as unattractive. I told her how much I loved seeing people of all sizes share photos of themselves in outfits that hugged curves and accentuated their shapes. I applauded them for being bold and unapologetic when it came to their bodies.

I smiled widely as I told Carrie that for the most part, I was bold and unapologetic when it came to my body, too. I wore whatever I wanted, and I never felt the need to hide. Even though it wasn't perfect, I loved my body. I wasn't like the insecure girls who stared at themselves in the mirror, wishing they could have different calves, or thighs, or shoulders. I had evolved past having such shallow concerns and learned to love myself exactly as I was.

Carrie did not clap for me or congratulate me for having so much confidence in a world that preys on the insecurities of women. She questioned whether I truly loved my body. She reminded me that my Black body had been the source of a lot of trauma in my life, social judgment, romantic rejection, emergency hospitalization, religious oppression, and sexual pressures. She asked me whether I had healed from all those painful experiences that were so intrinsically connected to my body, or whether I'd buried those emotions.

    I felt a lump in my throat. Tears welled up in my eyes as I contemplated Carrie's questions. She was right. My body was the source of a lot of trauma in my life and I hadn't processed through most of it. When I said that I loved body, what I really meant to say is that I loved the way my body looked.

    For years, the conversation I had with myself about loving my body was centered around loving what I saw when I looked in the mirror. I understand now that there's much more to my body than meets the eye. It is a vessel for my experience. It keeps score of what's happened to me, from the scar on my shoulder to the tension in my back. Paying attention to the story my body is telling me and the emotions flowing through it has helped me heal past a lot of the trauma in my life.

CHAPTER 32
SOPHIE SHORTS

Thanks to my dad, I grew up around basketball. In high school, Dad was the star of his basketball team. He would have loved to play basketball in college, but since he started his first year at Cornell University at just fifteen years old, he wasn't as strong or as developed as the other first year athletes.

Basketball remained an important part of Dad's life. He loved the Los Angeles Lakers, especially during the Magic Johnson era, his all-time favorite NBA player. He never missed a game. When he wasn't by a television, he tuned in to the radio to hear the announcers give the play-by-play. He cheered and clapped when the Lakers scored, and muttered words under his breath that I wasn't supposed to repeat when they lost.

I didn't really understand what was so great about throwing a ball through a net hoop, but I knew that Dad loved it, so I wanted to love it, too. I played in recreational leagues throughout elementary school, and I spent my summers at basketball camp. I was small, and I wasn't the most coordinated person, but I was fast, feisty, and dedicated. I never played like I was afraid, no matter how much bigger the girls were than I was. In my mind, I was always the biggest threat.

In the seventh grade, I joined a small recreational league basketball team shortly after my family moved to Manassas, Virginia. As he often did, Dad volunteered to help coach. The parents were ecstatic and gave him the head coaching job without delay. To this day I'm not sure why they allowed a perfect stranger, and a Black one at that, to come in and takeover, but I think they saw Dad as their own personal Magic Johnson. The team, which had been comprised of all White girls until I joined, had lost most of their games the previous year. I believe they thought my dad would help them turn things around.

As head coach Dad went back to the basics. We did layup drills and passing drills and dribbling exercises at every practice. When he felt like we were ready, we moved on to scrimmages and running plays. Slowly, the team's losing streak turned around, and by the end of the season, we had won half of our games.

By the time I reached the eighth grade, I was the star of my team. The other girls looked up to me to call the plays and to put points on the board, but more than anything, they looked to me for morale. I encouraged my teammates who were feeling defeated, and I jumped out of my seat cheering for them when they scored, just like I'd seen Dad do when I was a kid.

At thirteen years old, I wasn't just growing as a basketball player, but I was growing into a woman. First, I started my period. Then, seemingly overnight, the little mosquito bites on my chest turned into plums. My aunties smiled and gave me big hugs when they pointed out how much my "tatas" were growing, as if I had accomplished something important. I crossed my arms, attempting to hide the little plums on my chest. I wasn't comfortable with them yet, and I didn't like the idea of people staring at them.

I still remember the day Mom took me shopping at Macy's for my first bra. Since she's a doctor, she always speaks about the body very matter-of-factly. She told me that since I was now a woman, it was time to cover my breasts. I put my face in my hands as she rattled on about how sacred the woman's body was and how one day, I might decide to have a baby of my own.

We left Macy's an hour later with two small A-cup bras and a few small sports bras. I put my new sport bra on before basketball practice the next evening. I liked the way I looked in my sports bra. I felt like Sporty Spice. I pulled my t-shirt over my head and then ran downstairs to wait for Dad in the living room.

Mom was already downstairs waiting for me in the living room. I was surprised to see her sitting there on the couch and I wondered if she planned to come to practice with Dad and me. She usually came to our weekend games when she didn't have to round on patients at the hospital, but she never came to weekday practices.

"We need to talk, Kiki," she said. After her long talk about my breasts the night before, I knew where this was going. I assured her that my bra fit just fine, and that I didn't need a reminder why I needed to wear one. Running without a bra would be uncomfortable, and potentially distracting for people who watched.

Mom shook her head and said that it wasn't my bra she wanted to talk about. It was my shorts. I tilted my head in confusion.

Until that point, I had always gone to basketball practice in Sophie shorts, short cotton shorts with a white elastic band and small triangle slits on each side. I owned them in every color of the rainbow and often put bows in my hair to match. I wore them to dance practice, to ride bikes, to walk in the park, and even to bed.

Mom had never said anything to me about my shorts before, and I didn't know why she had a problem with them now. She clarified that it wasn't my shorts that were the problem, but the way they squeezed my butt. Apparently, my tatas weren't the only things that were growing.

She took my hand, walked me to the downstairs bathroom, and stood next to me in the mirror. She turned me to the side and made me look at my butt in the mirror. I admitted that my shorts were much tighter than I remembered them being before, but I didn't think it was a big deal. I was just going to basketball practice, not church. Most of the girls on my team wore small Sophie shorts, too.

"Well, you're not like all the girls," she said. She explained that I was Black, and even though I was small, my thighs and butt were bigger than the White girls on my team. That meant I couldn't get away with wearing what they wore. When they wore them, it was cute. When I wore them, it was sexy.

Mom feared my shorts might attract the wrong type of attention. She feared that the mothers would judge me unfairly, or that one of my teammates' fathers or brothers would say or do something sexually inappropriate. She also didn't want any of the older boys who practiced at the same gym to take advantage of me. In her mind, my shorts were a safety concern.

At thirteen years old, sex was the last thing on my mind. I had never even kissed a boy, and I had only stopped playing with Barbies the year prior. I was offended by her suggestion that I should change my shorts because of how other people might perceive me. It wasn't my fault that I was Black, or that I had a bigger butt than other girls.

Mom sighed. She still thought that I should change my shorts, but she wanted me to decide for myself. Annoyed, I stormed out of the bathroom and returned to the living room to wait for Dad. I hadn't done anything wrong, so I had no plan to change my clothes.

I was insecure about my Sophie shorts all night at practice. I pulled them down every few minutes, scanning the audience for watching eyes. I couldn't help but notice how differently my teammates' shorts fit them. They were much looser fitting than mine. I spent so much time and energy focusing on everyone's shorts that I started making careless mistakes and missing easy shots.

Feeling defeated, I told Dad I needed a water break. A few of the older boys who had been practicing in the neighboring gym were hanging out by the water fountain down the hall. With Mom's words echoing in my head, I made my way down the hall. My heart beat increased as I approached the fountain. Without saying a word to the boys, I bent over slightly to take a sip of water.

"Damn, she's got a fat ass!" one of them said from behind me. The other boys all laughed. My stomach dropped. I didn't know what to say. I couldn't tell whether the boys were paying me a compliment or just trying to make me feel uncomfortable. I went with the first. I turned around, smiled, and thanked him for the compliment. They all erupted in laughter.

I replayed that scene in my mind repeatedly as I lay in bed that night. Maybe Mom was right. Maybe I had no business wearing clothes that were too short or too tight. Maybe it was my job to make sure that I covered my body to avoid any unwanted attention. Or maybe it wasn't.

CHAPTER 33
PUT YOU TO BED

From Baby Phat to American Eagle, I experimented a lot with fashion throughout high school as I navigated my racial identity. I couldn't decide whether I wanted to look like TLC, Blake Lively, or Avril Lavigne. But no matter what I wore I was careful not to wear anything too short, too tight, or too revealing.

By high school I had learned that boys liked sex, and wearing sexy clothes made them think about having sex with you. I wasn't a prude by any means, but I definitely didn't want to be labeled with a Scarlett letter like Hester Prynne. If I ever hoped to get married, I had to protect my reputation as a good, wholesome girl. That meant I had to dress accordingly with no cleavage, no belly rings, no fish net stockings, no super short dresses, no lingerie, and no stripper heels.

I started college at the University of Virginia with the same mentality. I believed that as long as I dressed appropriately and made wise decisions, I'd be safe from sleazy guys and sexual predators. I packed up my closet full of sweaters, jeans, polos, and t-shirts and brought them with me to dorms.

A few weeks into our first semester, a few of the Superfriends and I went to a dance party at a venue down the street from our dorm. I wore blue jeans with a pink floral tank top and a pair of flip-flops. I knew we were going to have to walk at least half a mile to get there and I wanted to be comfortable.

I felt grossly under dressed when we arrived at the party. The older girls wore tight sparkly dresses, short leather skirts, low-cut bodysuits, and six-inch heels. They all looked so beautiful and confident, like movie stars. The boys thought so, too.

I looked down bashfully at my own flip flops. Suddenly, I felt unattractive in my jeans and floral tank top. I couldn't imagine that any of the boys would want to talk to me when they could talk to any number of the movie-star looking girls that were there.

I watched the sexy older girls dance and flirt as I stood with my friends in the corner. A part of me judged them for being so provocative. Another less pronounced but noticeably present part of me longed to look just like them. But I knew that dressing sexy would tempt boys to engage in sinful sexual acts, and I wasn't supposed to be a temptress. Feeling confused, I shoved the rising admiration down as deeply as I could.

After dancing with my friends in the corner for what felt like a much longer time than it probably was, I was approached by a good-looking and caramel skinned boy who asked me to dance. He had a warm smile and beautiful white teeth. He wore a crisp white t-shirt and smelled like fresh cedar wood. His request flattered me. There were lots of attractive women for him to choose from, but he was interested in me. Me, in my simple blue jeans and flip-flops.

I smiled and agreed to dance. He rested his large, warm hands comfortably on the small of my back as the music played. We were in a room packed full of people, but for a moment it felt like we were the only ones in the room.

I danced with the good-looking stranger for three songs

in a row. I liked being close to him. I didn't know his name or anything about him, but we had chemistry. I wondered if he'd ask for my number or offer to take me on a date when the night ended. I briefly considered the possibility that he could be my future husband. One day, I might tell our kids the story of how their father sought me out at a party and asked me to dance.

As the night wound down, the music slowed down too. Couples around the room held each other close as J. Holiday's, "Bed" began to play. I could see out of the corner of my eye that my friends were dancing with boys too.

The good-looking stranger pulled me in closer, unleashing an avalanche of emotions inside me. I didn't know whether what I felt was love, fear, or adrenaline, but I liked the rush. As we danced, I felt one of his hands slip around the front of my waist. Slowly, he lowered his hand into my pants. Taken aback by the sexual gesture, I froze.

"Stop," I whispered into his ear. He asked me what was wrong. His hand still lingered inside my jeans, his fingers fondling the most private part of my body. I clutched his wrist and slowly pulled his hand away from me. I told him that I didn't want to move too fast. After all, we had just met.

"Then why did you dance with me for so long?" he asked, his tone much harsher than it had been before. I told him I was sorry. For what I wasn't quite sure, but it was clear that something I had done had offended him. He asked if I planned to come home with him, and when I shook my head no, he rolled his eyes, muttered something about how I was a tease, and walked away without even asking for my name.

I stood there alone in the middle of the dance floor for a few seconds until I could bring myself to walk away. I was shocked. As far as I was concerned, I had done everything the way society had taught me to do to protect myself. I wasn't drunk, I wasn't dressed provocatively, and I had shown up to the party with a group of girlfriends. I didn't whisper sweet nothings into his ear or ask him back to my dorm. I was just a girl who said yes to a boy who asked to dance.

I didn't tell anyone what happened that night. I imagined the questions I'd get about what I had done to lead him to believe that I wanted to be touched. A part of me felt guilty. Maybe I had led him on by dancing with him for so long. Maybe I should have known that he would expect me to come home with him. I didn't know his name even if I wanted to report him.

I didn't realize it back then, but I later uncovered in a therapy session that I learned a valuable life lesson that night. It didn't matter whether I wore a conservative pair of jeans or a short leather mini skirt. There was nothing I could do to control the actions of men who had no intention of respecting my body.

CHAPTER 34
CATS AND DOGS

Even though we're ten years apart, my baby sister Nia is my best friend. I still remember the day my parents told me I was going to have a little sister. I jumped up and down on their bed shrieking in celebration. I loved my brother Johnathan, but I was ready for a sister. I wanted a mini me to dress up and have tea parties with. I got my wish.

Since the day my parents brought her home from the hospital, Nia and I have been inseparable. I've always felt like she was wise beyond her years. She is refreshingly easy to talk to, and one of the least judgmental people I've ever met. She's also an impressive singer and songwriter. At just seven years old, she used to sit at the old wooden piano in our dining room for hours composing songs about love, heartbreak, reflection, and regret.

Nia and I have a lot in common. We both entered the world at six pounds, twelve ounces. We both wear rings in our noses and switch up our hairstyles every few months. We both appreciate people with a dry sense of humor, and we both have a hard time waking up early in the morning. We both love ribeye steak, trips to Disney World, musical theater, and all things Harry Potter. We are also unquestionably loyal to the people we love.

There are also lots of differences between Nia and I. We often joke that I'm like a dog and she's more like a cat. I love hugs and cuddles and words of affirmation, while Nia is not keen on being touched. I'm confrontational, while Nia tries to avoid conflict. I love babies with chubby cheeks, while Nia thinks they look like aliens from a different planet. We also have very different tastes when it comes to fashion. I love ornate fur coats and frilly dresses, while Nia prefers jean jackets and combat boots.

Nia and I also have very different body types. I have always had a small, delicate frame. Growing up, I was often one of the most petite kids in class. My curves filled out nicely when I hit puberty, but I only moved up the clothing scale from a size 0 to a size 2. Although Nia is my little sister her curves have always been much more voluptuous than mine. When we go out together people often mistake Nia for my older sister. Usually we just smile and kindly correct them.

For the most part, nobody said anything to me about my size growing up. When people did comment on my body, they told me how lucky I was to be so small. Even grown women pined over my long, slender legs, and expressed how much they envied my metabolism.

I felt the most uncomfortable when people combined their compliments with self-deprecating comments. I never knew how to respond appropriately. Once, a woman I didn't know very well told me that she was never going to find love because, unlike me, she was fat and unattractive. If I'm honest, I did think the woman was overweight. I didn't want to unpack what she said because I was ashamed to admit that deep down, I believed overweight people were less attractive too. In an effort to avoid my own discomfort and shame, I smiled and assured her that she was beautiful just the way she was.

By the time Nia reached puberty, I was already in college. Her boobs did not grow to the size of plums like mine, but juicy mangoes. At just thirteen years old, she was more developed than I was. When we took pictures on the beach, she put me on her back instead of jumping on mine like she used to do as a kid.

Aside from our body types, Nia and I strongly favor one another. We both have big almond eyes, high cheekbones, and honey brown skin. This never worked in Nia's favor growing up because everyone felt the need to compare her to me.

Sometimes the comparisons people made were subtle. For example, our mom never told Nia that she should strive to look more like me, but she'd casually make comments in front of Nia about how cute and petite I was. She also made derogatory comments about her own body when she looked in the mirror. Each time, I cringed because she and Nia were about the same size. Although I don't believe Mom's intent was to make Nia feel bad about her body, the message she sent was clear. Smaller is better.

At other times, the comparisons people made between Nia and me were overt. When she was in middle school, Nia came home crying one day after a group of girls in her class made fun of her for living in my shadow. They had pulled up one of my pageant pictures online, and in front of the entire class asked her why there were no pictures of her on the internet. Everyone laughed.

I was furious when Mom called me at school to tell me about what happened. I hated that they made her feel like she wasn't good enough. I called Nia the next day to tell her how sorry I was. She cried as she recounted the story. She told me that when she looked at my pageant pictures, the ones that decorated the walls of our house, it made her feel like she wasn't skinny enough, or pretty enough. When she finished her story,

I reminded her that she was wonderfully made just the way she was. I couldn't tell whether she believed me, but she nonetheless thanked me for calling.

Another time, Nia told me that a family friend was giving her a hard time about her eating habits. The woman, who was three times Nia's age and almost twice Nia's size, made snarky comments every time Nia ate around her, and often compared Nia's body to mine. Nia said she always responded politely even though she really wanted to tell the woman off. I encouraged Nia to do her best to ignore it.

I should have told that woman to go to hell, but back then, I didn't have the tools I needed to adequately affirm or advocate for Nia. I spent years avoiding conversations about size and weight. I had never acknowledged the privilege that I wielded as a naturally thin woman and sitting in that privilege was hard. No one had ever made snarky comments about my eating habits or made fun of me for my weight. I had the privilege of moving through life without ever having to think about my size.

That year, Nia developed an eating disorder. She later told me that she ate as little as physically possible to lose weight. Some days, she ate as little as a piece of toast. As the captain of the basketball team, the track team, and the lacrosse team, she was burning far more calories than she consumed.

Nia was good at concealing her eating habits and even better at concealing her emotions. For the most part, she presented herself as the same happy-go-lucky girl she'd always been. She laughed at my jokes, hung out with her friends on the weekends, and practiced the piano in her free time. I knew that she had some insecurities about her body, but I didn't know the full extent to which she was struggling with her self-image.

One afternoon, my mother called me in a panic. She had just received a phone call from Nia's track coach. Nia's coach informed my mother that Nia had fainted in the middle of track practice. She was dehydrated and undernourished. My heart dropped.

I called Nia that evening to check on her, but she wasn't ready to talk about it. She was embarrassed. I was the last person she wanted to talk to about her body image. If anything, I was part of the reason people had given her a hard time about her size her entire life.

It wasn't until eight years later that Nia and I had an in-depth conversation about her eating disorder. She helped me understand how the pressure to be thin can impact both one's physical and mental health. Although I couldn't relate to feeling too big, I knew what it was like to feel too Black. If developing an eating disorder had carried the promise of making me less Black, it's likely I would have developed one too.

Hearing Nia talk about her experience growing up broke my heart. It forced me to think more critically about my own bias. I had to make a conscious effort to deconstruct the message I had received both from my mom growing up and from society that small bodies were more beautiful than big ones.

PART 11
DEATH BY CHOCOLATE

    I was talking to my Grandpa Joey on the phone a few months back about the murder of Ahmaud Arbery, an unarmed twenty-five-year-old Black male who was shot to death in February 2020 while jogging near his home in a neighborhood outside Brunswick, Georgia. Ahmaud was pursued by three White men, father and son Gregory McMichael and Travis McMichael, and their neighbor William "Roddie" Bryan. Travis McMichael shot Ahmaud three times with a shotgun while Bryan filmed the encounter. Travis McMichael later claimed he thought Ahmaud was a burglar, although he didn't have any concrete evidence other than the color of his skin.

    None of the men were charged by local police immediately after the shooting. They remained free until Bryan's video of Ahmaud's death was leaked on the internet three months later. The video went viral and fueled widespread outrage. In November 2021 jurors found all three men involved with the shooting guilty of nearly all the counts against them, including felony murder, aggravated assault, false imprisonment, and criminal attempt to commit a felony. The shooter, Travis McMichael, was also found guilty of malice murder.

I told Grandpa Joey what scared me the most was the idea that Ahmaud could have easily been my little brother Johnathan. Like Ahmaud, Johnathan has chocolate brown skin and an athletic build. As a husband, father, and pediatrician who works erratic hours at the hospital, working out helps him manage his stress. It's not uncommon for him to ride his bike early in the morning or go on an afternoon jog like Ahmaud. Johnathan has been racially profiled while jogging on many occasions, but luckily for him he's never been shot.

Grandpa Joey understood my fear. At six feet two inches, he has been racially profiled since he was a teenager. When he was a little boy White people smiled at him and told his mother how cute he was. When he became a man the smiles stopped. Women clutched their bags when he neared them, people locked their car doors when he walked past them on the sidewalk, and police harassed him without cause.

For Grandpa Joey, Ahmaud's story was all too familiar. Growing up in Newark, New Jersey in the '50s and '60s, he had known dozens of Ahmaud Arberys. For him, Ahmaud's death was a painful reminder of how hard it can be to be a young Black man in America.

CHAPTER 35
I GO TO UVA

Just a few weeks into my first year at UVA, I snuck into my first bar. It was a small pub close to campus in an area known as "The Corner". I was only eighteen, but I wasn't the only one there underage. Technically, all the bars on The Corner required patrons to be twenty-one years old, but in practice they were full of underage college students like me, many of whom were White.

On March 8, 2015, three White Alcoholic Beverage Control officers asked Black UVA student Martese Johnson for his ID outside of bar on the corner named Trinity. Martese was in his third year, and a friend of my little brother Johnathan. Like Johnathan, he was only twenty years old at the time.

According to the police records, Martese promptly showed the officers his ID. The officers responded by slamming Martese to the ground, bashing his head to the pavement and bloodying his face. One officer pinned him to the ground with his knee on his back and put him in handcuffs. Martese's classmates watched in horror as his blood painted the sidewalk.

The next morning, everyone at school was talking about

what happened to Martese. Thankfully, a by-stander captured everything on film. My heart pounded as I watched the video of the encounter on Instagram.

"His head is bleeding!" a young man yelled over and over. Still, the officers did not release their hold on Martese.

"I go to UVA!" Martese screamed in desperation. "How did this happen? I go to UVA!"

Martese was one of hundreds of underage UVA students out at bars that night, but none of the other students were brutally attacked. His injuries left him with bloody streaks that ran down his face, an image that quickly went viral on social media. People around the country were outraged. They couldn't believe that a smart, politically active college kid like Martese was treated so terribly. After all, he wasn't a weed-smoking troublemaker, he was a good kid.

Even I was shocked by the way Martese had been treated. I thought that going to UVA was a shield of protection against the racist, outside world. In fact, I elected to attend UVA, a prestigious, predominately White institution (PWI) instead of a historically Black university because of the social capital it would provide.

Most of the time, it works in my favor. White people often relate to me differently when they find out I graduated from UVA. They relax their shoulders, loosen their lips, and tell me stories about their friends, cousins, and sisters-in-law who are also UVA alumni.

I once had a dentist appointment with an old White man who barely looked me in the eye as I spoke. He gave one-word answers to all of my questions and dismissed all of my concerns. The grumpy dentist left the exam room halfway through the appointment, but when he came back there was a big smile on his face. "Why didn't you tell me you went to UVA?" he asked, his tone much brighter than it had been a few minutes earlier. He had seen it in on my intake paperwork when he went to check my dental records. He carried on about how great a school it was, and how his son hoped to graduate from UVA one day. He was much gentler with the dentist's tools in his hand after that.

Unfortunately for Martese, attending a PWI was not a shield of protection on the night they slammed his head into the concrete. In a *Vanity Fair* article following the incident, he expressed his belief that he always believed education and success would be his sanctuary. But when the officers saw his Black skin, they didn't treat him like a student full of potential like the hundreds of other White kids out on The Corner that night. They treated him like he was a criminal.

Unlike many other Black people who have had violent encounters with police officers, Martese Johnson lived to tell his story. What happened to Martese was a sobering reminder that no matter how much social capital I carry, there will always be someone to remind me that underneath it all, I am still Black. Shouting "I graduated with both a bachelors and doctorate degree from the University of Virginia!" may earn me special treatment at the dentist's office, but it may not enough to protect me in a life-threatening altercation with the police.

CHAPTER 36
BLACK LIVES MATTER

I have a particular disdain for the phrase "All Lives Matter." It's not because I don't believe that all lives matter. I believe all life does matter. In fact, even the lives of my mortal enemy's matter to me - not that I have any, but if I did, their lives would matter. After all, every good story requires an antagonist.

I hate the phrase "All Lives Matter" because whenever I see it used, it's being thrown around as a passive aggressive (or in many cases just aggressive) phrase to discredit the Black Lives Matter movement. The movement has been so crucified by conservative news media outlets you'd think it was the "*Only* Black Lives Matter" movement. It's completely gone over a good portion of American people's heads that the purpose of the movement is to remind people that Black Lives Matter, *too*.

The only phrase I hate more than All Lives Matter is "Blue Lives Matter." Again, it's not because I don't believe the lives of police officers, or "Blue Lives", don't matter. It's because the phrase is often rooted in the dismissal of the Black Lives Matter movement. I once asked a conservative friend whether she believed Black lives mattered and she responded, "Blue Lives

Matter", as if the opposite of a Black life is a "Blue" one.

America already knows that Blue lives matter. The lives of police officers are not only protected by weapons and bulletproof vests, but they're also shielded by policies and laws like qualified immunity and The Law Enforcement Officers' Bill of Rights. Nonetheless, every time a Black person dies at the hands of a police officer, some people feel the need to remind us all how important the life of the still-living police officer is.

I had a few friends back home in Virginia who worked as police officers, but we never had genuine conversations about racism or the state of policing in America. Although we talked about their jobs occasionally, the conversations were always surface level. I'd ask them how work was and they'd tell me about the latest person they arrested or the craziest thing they'd seen. We didn't have in-depth conversations about racism or police brutality. I was afraid to go down that road in fear of how it would affect our relationship, and deep down I think they were too.

The death of Trayvon Martin was particularly controversial in my hometown of Manassas. The neighborhood watch volunteer who shot him, George Zimmerman, grew up in Manassas and graduated from my high school six years before me. Lots of people from home jumped to his defense, including a handful of my police officer friends. I didn't agree with them, but I understood why it might have been hard for them to speak out against Zimmerman.

Following the murder of George Floyd by a White police officer Derek Chauvin in 2020, the racial climate across the country was unusually thick. True to form, the Blue Lives Matter people did everything they could to discredit and dismiss the Black Lives Matter people, but something about this murder felt different. Usually, I tried my best to see things from the opposite perceptive. Maybe the officer was scared. Maybe they really did believe they saw a gun. But when I watched the video of Chauvin with his knee pinned to Floyd's neck, I didn't see an officer in fear of his life. I saw a monster, a man who did not believe Floyd's Black life mattered.

Still, people defended Chauvin. My social media was again inundated with posts hash tagged #BlueLivesMatter. Ironically, this time I noticed my police officer friends from back home, the ones who had come to George Zimmerman's defense years prior, posted nothing. They remained silent in the days that followed. They posted nothing in defense of Floyd. Nothing in defense of Chauvin.

I wasn't sure what I had expected, but somehow their silence was even worse than the loud support for Chauvin. At least I knew where those people stood. At least I knew the video had affected them. I wondered if any of my police officer friends felt anything at all when they watched the life drain from Floyd's body.

At this point, I was living in Los Angeles and hadn't spoken to any of my police officer friends in almost five years, but I wanted to know how they felt about Floyd's death. I wondered what went through their minds as they watched Chauvin pin his knee on Floyd's neck. I wondered whether they believed Chauvin's actions were justified, or if they too saw a monster when they looked at him.

Out of a mix of overwhelming curiosity and growing frustration, I called my friend Isaac. Isaac was an old friend from church who had been working as a police officer for years. Out of all my police officer friends, Isaac and I were the closest. We had the same sense of humor, and the same taste in music. There was a time when he told me all his secrets and I told him mine.

Isaac was always far more socially conservative in his beliefs than I was. We generally avoided conversations about politics and elections. Nonetheless, I trusted him to have an honest conversation with me about George Floyd. I knew that at the very least, he'd tell me truth.

He was happy to hear from me. We slipped back into our old patterns with ease. We exchanged stories about our jobs, our loved ones, and our new favorite songs. He told me about funny things his kids had done, and about the new tattoo he planned to get. I surprised him when I told him I had a tattoo now, too.

When I could tell we both felt safe, I shifted the conversation. Without any pretext, I asked Isaac whether he believed Black lives mattered. After years of friendship, I knew he cared about me as a person, but I needed to know that I wasn't just the exception.

Isaac took a deep breath. He knew where the conversation was headed. "Yes, Black lives matter," he said. "George Floyd's life mattered." I let out a small sigh of relief.

I asked Isaac what he thought about the police officer who killed George Floyd. This time, he lingered a bit before responding. He admitted that it broke his heart to see Derek Chauvin kneeling on Floyd's neck. He said he believed most cops were good people with good intentions, but just like in any organization, there were officers who abused the badge. Even within his own agency, he knew racist officers who took advantage of the power they wielded.

The corners of my lips curled up into a slight smile. In the many years that I had known Isaac, I had never heard him talk about racism, social justice, or police brutality. I asked him why he didn't say any of those things publicly. People would listen to him. He wasn't just a police officer, he was a husband, a father, a friend, and a community leader. He could tell people that Black lives mattered, and they might believe him. As a police officer, it would mean something different coming out of his mouth.

Isaac explained that it wasn't as simple as I made it sound. It was much more complicated than most people understood. There was a sound of rehearsed defeat in his voice as he spoke as if he'd had this same conversation with himself a thousand timed before.

He feared how his fellow police officers would respond if he posted something online as controversial as "Black lives matter". Many of them equated supporters of the Black Lives Matter movement with domestic terrorism. They internalized critiques of the policing system as personal attacks on their Whiteness and their character.

Isaac couldn't afford to lose respect or credibility amongst his peers. He worried that speaking out might cost him his job, or even worse, his life. As a police officer, he depended on his fellow officers to have his back in life-threatening situations.

He also feared how speaking out would affect his relationships with his friends and family. Many of the people we knew back home saw the Black Lives Matter movement as anti-Christian and anti-American. In addition to likely being ostracized at work, he would risk being socially ostracized if he said anything to support the movement. While I had moved across the country and made lots of new liberal friends, Isaac was still living with the ultra-conservative people we grew up with.

I thanked Isaac for being honest with me and told him I understood why he was hesitant to share his opinion publicly. I had never considered the backlash Isaac might face for speaking out. I also shared how much it would mean to me as his friend, and as a Black woman, if he would use his voice on behalf of the Black community anyway. I reassured him that if he found the courage to use his voice, I would support him however I could. Although he was afraid, he wasn't alone.

I didn't know if anything would come from my conversation with Isaac, but I was thankful for the opportunity to explain how I felt, and I was even more thankful he cared enough to listen. I also had a better understanding of his perspective. I understood that for Isaac, his silence was not a product of apathy, but of fear.

I was shocked when my brother Johnathan called the next afternoon to tell me that Isaac had made a long post about George Floyd's murder on Facebook. Immediately, I opened the Facebook app on my phone and searched his page. I smiled when I came across the words, "Black lives matter." Just as Isaac feared, there were several people in the comment section who expressed disappointment in the stance he took, but there were far more people who said that his willingness to stand up for what he believed in was inspiring.

By the end of the day, Isaac's post was the talk of the town. It may not have been enough to inspire a complete overhaul of the system, but it was a damn good start.

CHAPTER 37
LAW AND ORDER

One afternoon, my boss took my co-workers and me to lunch at a chic restaurant down the street from our downtown Hollywood office. My boss, Louis, was a middle-aged White man with an impressive resume and a lot of money. He and his family lived in a large house in the Westside of Los Angeles, one of the most expensive neighborhoods in town.

Louis and I were very different. We didn't have the same taste in food, music, or movies, and we spent our time outside of work very differently. He spent most of his weekends golfing or socializing at his private water-front beach club with his wife and young daughter. I couldn't even pronounce the names of the restaurants where he liked to dine.

I often spent my weekends cleaning, doing laundry, or running errands. Unlike Louis, I didn't have a nanny or a housekeeper to help around the house. At night, I spent time with my friends or lounged on my living couch binging the latest Netflix series. When I was feeling particularly fancy, I ordered a meal on Uber Eats instead of heating up a pack of Ramen noodles from my pantry.

Although we didn't have much in common, I thought of Louis as a father figure. He advocated for me at work and was a constant source of support and life advice. Some days I sat in his office while he told me stories about his life. He talked about his childhood, his best friend growing up, and his wild college days. His life fascinated me, and I clung to every word of every story, the way small children cling to their parents when they cross the street.

At our team lunch that afternoon one of my co-workers shared that he was going to Mexico for the weekend. Naturally we were all jealous. There were several popular vacation destinations in Mexico within driving distance of Los Angeles. It was the perfect place for a weekend getaway.

Our lighthearted conversation about weekend getaways morphed into a heavy conversation about Mexican immigrants at the border. President Trump had recently cracked down on his immigration policy leading to devastating separations between American children and their immigrant parents. The troubling images we saw on the television news of hysterical parents and crying children in cages deeply disturbed most of us.

My boss Louis was less empathetic towards the Mexican immigrants than the rest of us. He said they were on American territory illegally, so it made logical sense to send them home, and if they wanted to live in America they needed to go through the proper channels. I rolled my eyes at this.

None of us were persuaded by his argument, so Louis continued to make his case. My blood boiled as he continued to speak. He reminded us that the immigrants had broken the law, and as lawyers we should understand that breaking the law was bad. We had to enforce laws if we wanted to maintain order in society.

Upset by Louis's cold rationalization, I reminded him that he had broken the law on several occasions in the past. He drank alcohol before he turned twenty-one and smoked weed long before it was legal. Unlike many of the Mexican immigrants who crossed the border to give their families better lives, Louis broke the law for fun.

Louis turned red. He knew I was right. He reasoned that while he had technically broken the law in the past, the laws he broke were inconsequential. They had little, if any, effect on our nation. On the other hand, immigration was a matter of national security and had a considerable impact on our economy.

"What about slavery?" I snapped back. At this one of my co-workers almost choked on his lunch. Louis's red skin grew hotter. "At one point slavery was legal. Was that a law we should have followed?"

"Touché," Louis responded. No one else said a word. I'd won my case.

Like my boss Louis, I understand why modern societies need laws. Laws keep order and diminish chaos. However, as a Black person in America, I do not believe that all the laws we have in place are either good or moral. And given the history in America, why should I? Society was set up to make sure that wealthy White men like my boss were allowed to live above, not within, the confines of, rules, laws, and standards. In contrast, the laws were never intended to work in favor of Black people.

Historically, White Americans have used the law to oppress Black people. For hundreds of years, the law allowed White slave owners to enslave, rape, beat, whip and lynch Black people. According to the US Constitution of 1787, Black people were only counted as equivalent to 3/5ths of a White person for the purpose of representation in Congress, and this remained the law until the Constitution was amended after the Civil War.

Laws also kept Black people from learning how to read and write, from engaging in the American political process, and from acquiring wealth. Today, the law and more importantly its discriminatory application continue to systematically oppress people of color. Mass incarceration, taxes, public education, and healthcare policies disproportionately affect Black people.

Every day we're all given the opportunity to decide whether we will live a life that we design or desire, or a life that we default to. Part of designing our lives critically is by examining the laws that we are expected to follow. For many Black people the laws of our land are not sacred rulings to blindly revere, but guidelines that we must assess and question as individuals and as a society. From the abolition of slavery to the Civil Rights Act, every social revolution in America that has benefited Black people has centered on the abolishment of a law.

PART 12
NOT SO URGENT CARE

My Grandpa Joey doesn't trust doctors. He second guesses every diagnosis and often gets second and third opinions. He writes down everything the doctors tell him in a little notebook that he carries with him everywhere he goes. He figures that if he ever has to sue a doctor or a hospital, he'll have a better case if he has documented evidence.

Grandpa Joey isn't alone in his distrust of doctors. Black people's distrust of healthcare professionals dates back to the historical abuses of slaves by White doctors for medical experimentation. Documented evidence shows that this abuse was continued through the civil rights era.

It is well documented that for many years, researchers performed experiments on Black people based in part on the idea that Black bodies are more resistant to pain than White bodies. In 1932, a group of government scientists began a study of young Black men with syphilis which became known as the "USPHS Syphilis Study at Tuskegee". The men were told they were getting free treatment for their condition from the government. Unbeknownst to the men in the study, the treatments were placebos. The doctors had no intention of treating them. They were studying the effects of untreated syphilis. This study lasted forty years.

It doesn't end there. Historically, many Black women who were admitted to the hospital for completely different reasons were sterilized by doctors without their consent. According to Rebecca Kluchin, an assistant professor of History at California State University, these procedures came to be known as "Mississippi appendectomies." The women were told that they needed to get their appendix out, but instead they were sterilized.

My mom was a doctor when I was growing up, so unlike a lot of the Black people I know I trusted the healthcare system. I reasoned that just like there are bad teachers and bad police officers, there are bad doctors. It wasn't until I grew older and had my own nightmare experiences at the hospital that I realized the mistreatment of Black people by healthcare professionals is not just an exaggerated myth perpetrated by people like my Grandpa Joey.

CHAPTER 38
BLACK SKIN, WHITE COATS

I was sitting in the living room of our Manassas home doing homework one evening when my mom walked through the door. It was almost 9:00 p.m., which was late even for her. Most nights, she made it home by 8:00 p.m.

My mom Anastasia was a pediatrician with her own practice in old town Manassas. Her practice was the most popular pediatrician office in town. She took care of half of my friends, as well as most of the kids in our neighborhood. Her patients loved her. She was highly credentialed, personable, and funny.

That evening Mom's light brown eyes were heavy, and she moved much slower than usual. She put down her bag and then greeted me with a kiss on my forehead. I told her that Dad had made spaghetti earlier that evening and had left her a plate in the fridge. I watched her shuffle around the kitchen as she heated up a plate and poured herself a glass of wine.

"Why did you become a doctor?" I asked Mom as she sat at the table devouring her spaghetti. I wondered if she regretted choosing a profession that demanded so much of her time and energy.

She paused for a moment before she responded. I expected her to give a speech about how she wanted to help people, but she didn't.

"If I'm honest, I was brainwashed from a very early age by my dad, your granddad," she laughed, still focused on the plate of spaghetti on front of her. She told me that when she was a kid, she dreamed of owning her own toy store, but her dad wasn't having it.

Lots of Haitian parents in America only present two career options to their children. They can become a doctor or a lawyer. They want the sacrifices they made to give their children a better life to be worth it. Having a child who is a doctor or lawyer is the greatest honor and gives them bragging rights in the Haitian community.

My granddad wanted my mom to be a doctor. He convinced her that there was no better job than that of a doctor. Doctors made good money, and they earned respect even from White people. He impressed upon her how proud he would be to have a doctor for a daughter. By the time she went to middle school, she was sold on the idea. She never looked back.

I asked Mom if she was happy with her decision to become a doctor. She spent years of her life dedicated to reaching her goal, and she missed out on lots of moments with my siblings and me. She didn't bake cookies for the PTA bake sale or accompany our class on field trips to apple orchards. She was always in class or at work.

She took a break from slurping her spaghetti and smiled at me. She said that she loved my siblings and me very much, but that she also loved her job. She explained that she loved science. It made sense to her, and it helped her make sense of the world around her. Everything had an explanation, and every problem was solvable.

She also loved using science to help make people's lives better. She loved watching her patients grow from babies to young adults. She celebrated milestones with them and their families. She cried with them when they lost their grandparents or found out they had cancer. She celebrated with them when they got into their dream colleges or landed their first jobs. She was more than just their doctor, she was a constant stable presence in their lives. To many of her patients she was like family.

Back then, Manassas was predominately a White town. I had a hard time believing that Mom's White patients saw her as part of their families. I asked her if it was hard being a Black doctor in a town like Manassas, and if she felt like her White families respected her.

She explained that a lot of her White families were comfortable with having a Black pediatrician for their children, even if they were racist or wouldn't see a Black doctor themselves. From slavery to the civil rights era, Black women in America have a history of taking care of White children. For example, in a 2017 paper published in the *Journal of Southern History* entitled "Mothers' Milk: Slavery, Wet-Nursing, and Black and White Women in the Antebellum South," authors West and Knight discuss how during slavery, some White women even let their slaves breastfeed their children.

My mom believed that for some of her White families, having a Black pediatrician was like having a Black wet-nurse with a degree. I had never considered it from that perspective before, but it made sense. Although Mom was a doctor, she was still taking care of White people's children.

"There was this one time that someone in town called me a nigger doctor though," she added as she took a sip of her wine. She said it without a hint of pain, like she was recounting a pleasant childhood memory. I was shocked.

She explained that not everyone in town was happy about the fact that she started her own practice. She originally moved to Manassas to work at an office owned by an old White man, but after a year of working for him, she decided to start her own medical practice. In less than three months and with the help of my dad, she created a business plan, found an office location, bought the medical equipment, hired staff, and opened the doors to her practice. Her schedule was full the very first day.

She told me that the other doctors in town began to chat about her rapid success. They had a hard time believing that a young Black female physician could be doing so well for herself so early on in her career.

Despite the turmoil of that early time, Mom kept going. She was determined to prove to herself and everyone else that she belonged. By the grace of God her practice not only grew, but it also blossomed. A year after opening her own practice she was named the top pediatrician in Manassas. She eventually went on to become one of the top-rated doctors in Virginia.

"When people think about racism in the medical profession, they often think about Black patients, but they rarely consider how racism affects Black doctors," Mom explained. I looked at her with a new sense of pride as I watched her finish her spaghetti. She wasn't just a doctor, she was a fighter, and I believed in what she was fighting for.

CHAPTER 39
SILENT SCREAMS

    I lay in bed with my eyes closed covered by a thick white blanket, but I was in too much pain to sleep. Sweat dripped from my forehead, which made no sense because I was shivering. I closed my eyes and curled up into a ball in response to the stabbing pain in my uterus. I had cramped many times before, but this was different.

    It had been less than twenty-four hours since I'd been released from the emergency room, and the hospital was the last place I wanted to go. I forced myself to take a nap, thinking I'd feel much better after I rested. But the pain got worse.

    The stabbing pain I felt in my uterus was so sharp that I could barely move. I threw up all over my bedroom floor before I could make it to bathroom. I reached for my phone and called my parents as I lay sprawled across the floor.

    "Something is wrong," I said as soon as my parents picked up, my uterus now contracting even more intensely. I could barely form any words, and the room now felt like it was spinning. Tears streamed down my face. A part of me believed I was dying, and I was scared to die alone.

My parents insisted I return to the emergency room. I was in no shape to drive, so my brother ordered me an Uber. After confirming that the Uber was on the way, my mom asked me what I was wearing. I told her that I was in sweatpants and an old white shirt.

"You have to change Kiki," she said in a stern voice.

"I can't," I said. I was in too much pain. I shed another tear.

For some people it may come as a shock that my mom was concerned with the way I was dressed when I was in so much pain, but I understood her question. To a lot of health care professionals a poorly dressed Black person screams poverty, and poor Black patients are much less likely to receive quality care. Even though I didn't have the energy to change my clothes, I knew from my experience in the ER the night before that my mom was justified in her concern, so I did manage to change.

The night before, I went to the ER wearing the same sweat pants and old t-shirt. I told the on-call doctor, a young White male, about the sharp pain I was experiencing in my uterus. Initially, he had suggested that I just go home and sleep it off, but after examining the employer box on my intake form, he changed his advice.

"Why didn't you tell me you were a lawyer?" he asked. The excitement in his voice really bothered me. "I guess that means I have to keep you alive, then." He looked at me and laughed lightheartedly, as if he expected me to laugh too. I didn't think it was funny. Then he sent me to the ER.

The second doctor who examined me in the ER that first night also ignored my pain. After I had been sitting for hours in the waiting room, he examined me for a few minutes and then concluded that I was just fine. I told him that I thought something was wrong, but he dismissed my concerns. Without running any tests, he gave me some painkillers and sent me home alone.

My family stayed on the phone with me as my Uber made

its way to the hospital. I kept my hand over my mouth trying to keep from throwing up all over the backseat. When we arrived at the ER, I stumbled to the check-in counter and told the receptionist I needed to see a doctor right away.

The receptionist barely looked up from behind the counter and asked me for my ID and insurance card. My arms shaking, I pulled the requested cards out of my purse and put them in front of her. In return, she handed me a large stack of papers. She told me that if I wanted to be seen I needed to fill out all the forms.

I could barely stand up much less fill out any paperwork. I tried to explain as best as I could that I had just left the hospital a few hours prior, and I needed to be re-admitted immediately. I slurred my words as I held on to the counter for support.

"Rules are rules," she said as she typed behind the desk. Her face was stoic, lacking any sort of empathy or emotions. Before I could get another word out, I threw up on the counter.

Everything that happened next was a blur. A cold floor. Bright lights. White coats. A bed. IVs. And then finally sleep.

I woke up a few hours later to a White man hovering over me with a clipboard. He told me that I had a serious infection in my uterus, and he was glad that I came in when I did. He said that my infection could have led to infertility. He said if I had waited any longer, it could have turned into sepsis, and I could have died.

I let his words sink in. Infection. Infertility. Death.

My parents flew out to Los Angeles and came to the hospital the next morning. Things got better the moment they showed up. When the doctors and nurses found out that my mom was a doctor, they made sure I was treated well. They spoke to me with more compassion and checked on me more frequently. When I told them I was in pain they didn't ignore me. After three days of treatment, they sent me home.

Later that week I called my friend Camy, a Black nurse

who worked in the Los Angeles hospital system, to tell her about my nightmare experience. I told her all about the doctors and receptionists who dismissed my pain. My experience horrified Camy, but she said that sadly, she wasn't surprised. She knew lots of Black people who'd had similar experiences at the hospital.

She explained that at hospitals in the predominately White neighborhoods of Los Angeles like the one I frequented, there was often an assumption that Black people in the ER are poor, homeless, or drug addicts who were over exaggerating their pain. She said that when I showed up out of sorts the first time wearing just sweatpants and a t-shirt, they probably thought I was a poor Black girl looking for drugs or a place to stay for the night.

I sighed, discouraged by Camy's words. I wanted to call the hospital and yell at someone, anyone. I wanted to file a complaint and write a letter to the *Los Angeles Times* calling for a boycott of the hospital. But who would listen to me? What proof did I have other than my testimony? The only thing I could think about was my mom's advice to change my clothes. She was right. Wearing sweatpants and an old t-shirt to the ER that second time could have killed me.

CHAPTER 40
THE SONG THAT NEVER ENDS

I sat anxiously in the waiting room. "Ky-air-uh?" a nurse called out. I raised my hand, grabbed my bag, and followed behind her. She led me to an examination room and told me the doctor would be with me shortly.

The doctor was tall and slender with pale skin and cold hands. She performed a quick inspection and asked me questions about how I was recovering after my recent trip to the ER. Her questions were brief, and her tone was transactional. After asking me about my pain levels and my appetite, she brought up birth control. She asked me if I was interested in getting on the pill.

I told her that I wasn't interested in getting on the pill. I had tried taking Ortho Tri-Cyclen when I was younger, but I didn't like it. The doctor frowned at this. She tried to convince me to try a different brand like Yaz or Seasonale, but I wasn't interested.

Next, the doctor asked whether I was interested in another form of birth control like a NuvaRing, or a patch. I told her that I wasn't interested in any form of birth control. She frowned again and asked me why I wasn't interested.

I did not want to have to explain myself. The doctor was a stranger to me. Apart from the questions she had asked me moments prior and the information in my chart, she didn't know anything about me. Instead of offering an explanation, I reiterated that I was not there to discuss birth control. This was supposed to be a follow-up appointment for the infection I had been treated for.

The doctor frowned for a third time. She explained that without birth control, I was at risk of getting pregnant. I tried hard no to roll my eyes as she lectured me about the responsibility of having children.

"I'm twenty-seven years old," I reminded her. "I fully understood the risks of having unprotected sex."

"Do you really think you're going to be able to keep your legs closed?" she asked.

Her question made me feel dirty and ashamed. I wanted to cry. I wanted to tell the doctor that what I did with my body and who I had sex with was none of her business. I wanted to tell her that her tone and her comments were offensive and unacceptable. I wanted to demand that she let me speak to her supervisor.

But after my traumatizing experience at the hospital the previous week, I didn't have the energy to respond the way I wanted to. I was physically and emotionally exhausted. I was tired of fighting with receptionists and doctors. Instead of fighting with the presumptuous female doctor, I calmed my breath and responded to her question.

I explained that while I had no intention of having a baby any time soon, I was more than capable of taking care of a child. I told her that I was a lawyer, and that if I got pregnant, I would be financially prepared.

Like all the doctors the week prior, the doctor apologized, explaining that she didn't realize I was a lawyer. Apparently, she had missed that detail in my chart. I hated that I had to pull the lawyer card. I was tired of having to rattle off my professional qualifications to earn respect.

The doctor asked me a few more questions and then scurried out of the examination room. I wondered if she treated all her patients the way she treated me, or if she'd ask the next woman whether she could keep her legs closed. Moments later the nurse told me I was free to leave.

As I drove home that afternoon, I thought about all the things I could do to punish that doctor. I could make a formal complaint to her boss. I could write a letter to the hospital board. I could write to the local newspaper about my experience. Maybe they'd let her go, or maybe she'd lose her license.

But I decided that none of those things would make me feel any better. After all, it wasn't revenge that I wanted. It was respect.

PART 13
GUMBO AND HAPPY MEALS

Until I moved to Los Angeles in my mid-twenties, my diet consisted largely of fast food and Ramen noodles. My friends and coworkers in Los Angeles didn't eat Taco Bell or Burger King. They approached carbs with skepticism and abhorred sugar like it was the devil. In half of the restaurants we attended, the food was plant based, and milk alternatives were the standard. I topped Starbucks lattes off with almond, coconut, or oat milk.

My friends in LA jokingly made fun of my "basic palette." Salads and green vegetables reminded me of rabbit food, and just the idea of tofu made me nauseous. I refused to try Impossible Burgers because I couldn't stomach the idea of eating fake meat, and I stayed away from foods I couldn't pronounce, like gnocchi pasta and acai berries.

After we started dating, Michael often commented on my eating habits. Like many of my friends who had grown up in LA he was committed to healthy eating, and he encouraged me to eat foods with organic ingredients and limit my sugar and dairy intake.

One afternoon, I was frying a grilled bologna and cheese sandwich when Michael nonchalantly brought up a book he'd been reading, *How Not to Die* by Michael Greger, M.D. The book detailed how we eat directly affects the way our bodies perform. He explained that processed foods like white bread, bologna and cheese often contained large amounts of hidden fats and sodium and could contribute to long-term sicknesses and diseases.

"You really don't need to be eating all that cheese," he said.

I scooped up the grilled cheese with the spatula in my hand and slammed it on to the white plate sitting next to the stove. Noticing the shift in my mood, he asked me what was wrong. Before I could respond, tears spilled from eyes, splashing onto the sandwich in my hand.

Michael explained that he was just concerned about my eating habits and assured me that he didn't mean to offend me, but the more he spoke, the more upset I became. I had grown up eating bologna and grilled cheese sandwiches, and his comments felt like more than just an attack on my sandwich. They felt like an attack on my upbringing and a judgment of my past.

What Michael said wasn't wrong, but I would have liked him to consider there are many reasons other than health that people choose certain foods. I believe that food is more than just a means of survival. It is its own language. The food we eat tells a story. It tells the story of our cultures, our family traditions, our dysfunctions, and even our fears.

When I turned thirty-one, I started taking my food choices more seriously. I decided to start making choices that would improve my quality of life. Making changes to my diet wasn't easy. Letting go of certain eating habits made me feel like I was turning my back on who I used to be. However, the result was a healthier, happier version of me.

CHAPTER 41
FAST FOOD LOVE AFFAIR

One evening I was eating dinner with a girlfriend at Nobu, a restaurant in Los Angeles known for its haute cuisine and pricey dishes, when I spotted a family with four small children who looked to be between the ages of two and six sitting across the room. They all had the same fair skin and thin nose, and they were all dressed like they'd just left a Ralph Lauren photoshoot. I watched as the children devoured the plates of sushi, seafood, and fancy meats spread across the table.

I wondered how expensive the family's bill would be as I watched the smallest child pick up a piece of sushi with his bare hand and put the entire piece into his mouth. My friend and I had already spent over $200 for much less food. I couldn't fathom spending hundreds of dollars on a meal for toddlers.

I grew up on grilled cheese, hot dogs, bologna sandwiches, fried chicken, and Ramen noodles. Since my mom and dad were students, we didn't have a lot of money for fancy meals. I never felt poor though. I had never been exposed to expensive foods like steak and lobster, so I didn't know what I was missing. In fact some of my best memories are of eating bologna and cheese sandwiches on the living room floor of our small Charlottesville apartment while watching *Nick Jr.* on the small television we all shared.

Then still a medical student, Mom rarely stepped foot in the kitchen. She didn't have the time, the emotional bandwidth, or the desire to cook. If it wasn't for my dad we probably would have starved. When we were hungry, we called "Daddy!" Even now I can always count on my dad to whip up something that will make me smile.

Although Mom wasn't much of a chef we had our own food traditions. When my little brother and I were on good behavior, she'd take us to Burger King, just like her dad had done for her when she was a little girl. Her favorite meal at Burger King was the Whopper, so naturally, the Whopper became my favorite meal at Burger King too.

My dad and I had our own fast-food traditions. He introduced me to my favorite restaurant to this day, Taco Bell. Even though I was a thin child and had a small appetite, I could eat three, four, and sometimes five tacos at a time. Soft tacos. Hot tacos. Tacos Supreme. I loved all of them.

When I was seven years old, I woke up one night with tears streaming down my little brown cheeks. I ran to my parents and woke them up with urgency. Concerned, Dad sat up in the bed and flipped on the light. Both he and Mom asked me what was wrong.

"I had a dream," I began, attempting to get my words out between my tearful gasps for air. "I had a dream I was eating a taco. And then… I woke up." Mom rolled her eyes at this revelation and melted back into the bed, but Dad was amused. He swiped the tears from my cheek and said he was sorry that I had such a bad dream. He took me to Taco Bell the next afternoon.

On special occasions, Dad would pick up a bucket of KFC fried chicken for dinner. I ran to the kitchen as soon as the smell made its way down the narrow halls of our Charlottesville apartment. I loved the seasoned, crispy skin and the warm buttery biscuits.

As a kid, I never understood why fried chicken was a food that was stereotypically associated with Black people. People of all races, ages, and sizes loved fried chicken. Even today my White American friends, my Vietnamese friends, my Korean friends, my Latino friends, and my Black friends all love fried chicken.

Although my family loved eating fried chicken at home, Mom taught us that eating fried chicken in public as a Black person was unacceptable. If White people saw us eating fried chicken, it would confirm all the other bad stereotypes about Black people, too. They might believe we were dumb, lazy, and violent.

For the most part, I followed the "no fried chicken in public" rule. When the high school cafeteria served fried chicken for lunch, I ate pizza from the a la carte line instead. I didn't want to risk being stereotyped or made fun of by my White peers.

However, in my first year of college I broke the fried chicken rule. I picked up a plate of fried chicken and macaroni and cheese from the cafeteria between classes. I didn't have time to go back to my dorm to eat, so I decided to eat at one of the courtyards on campus instead. I sat by myself at a small table in the corner of the courtyard and began to eat.

As I ate my fried chicken, I spotted a group of White girls from my next class across the courtyard. One of them waved to me. Instinctively, I stopped eating my chicken and quickly closed the Styrofoam container with my food inside. When the girls reached me, they asked if they could sit with me. I smiled and told them I would be delighted.

The girls pulled Caesar salads, turkey sandwiches, and cold pizza out of their lunch bags. Suddenly I was ashamed of the fried chicken in the Styrofoam container in front of me. I couldn't stand the thought of eating the chicken in front of them, so I didn't. I watched them finish eating their lunches, and went to class.

CHAPTER 42
BAKED BRIE

"I'm going to the grocery store to get some food," Liza announced as she walked into the common room, tucking her long brown hair behind her ear. The common room was my favorite place in the old nunnery turned temporary housing. The ceiling was high, and all four walls were made from stone. The room was decorated with small wooden tables, antique lamps, and a weathered brown leather sofa.

It was January of 2010, and I was in Prato, Italy, studying abroad with a group of twenty-one other students from UVA. There were three Black people in our group, me included. The rest of the students were all White. Most of the White students already knew one another. Although we all went to the same school, I had never even seen most of them before our trip.

It was cold outside that evening, and even though I was comfortable in the warm, dimly lit common room, I couldn't ignore the rumbling noise coming from my stomach. I was too hungry to stay behind. I told Liza that I'd be happy to come with her to the grocery store. A few of the other girls in our class volunteered to come, too.

I grabbed my green tweed jacket and white wool hat and threw my black cross body bag over my shoulder. I didn't have much cash left in my bag. Between all the pizza, pasta, and gelato I had eaten over the past few weeks, I had spent more money on food in Italy than I had anticipated.

I followed Liza and the other girls down the cobbled streets. I loved the architecture in Prato. I appreciated the statues and the mini motorcycles which almost looked like they were made specially for the narrow Italian roads. I smiled at the bikers who passed by and at the old men sitting in the park. It all felt like a scene from *The Lizzie McGuire Movie*.

When we arrived at the grocery store a few blocks down I was overwhelmed by all the food options. The foods felt both familiar and foreign. I didn't recognize a lot of the packaging, and most of the signs and labels were written in Italian. I only knew a few words in Italian and none of them were helpful.

Eventually I settled for a pack of Ramen noodles. Ramen noodles held a special place in my heart. According to my dad, my mom ate a lot of Ramen noodles when she was pregnant with me, and as a young child it was one of my favorite lunch foods. When I went away to college, it became a staple part of my diet. At just fifteen cents a pack, it was the perfect meal for a poor college student.

When we ran into one another at the checkout line, Liza teased me about the pack of Ramen noodles in my hand. She couldn't believe that when we were in a foreign country most known for its cuisine, I was ready to settle for a pack of Ramen. I shrugged at her comments. I was hungry and I knew that it was guaranteed I would like the pack of noodles in my basket.

But Liza didn't want to hear it. She couldn't stomach the idea of watching me eat Ramen while everyone else ate much more refined foods. She insisted I put the Ramen back and share her meal instead. I didn't understand why what I chose to eat mattered to her so much.

Realizing that I was probably going to lose the battle, I asked Liza what she planned to eat for dinner. She perked up and gloated that she was going to make baked brie with a fig spread, paired with a dry Italian red wine. After the brie she planned to eat a crème brûlée she had found in the bakery.

Liza may as well have been speaking Italian. Apart from the wine, I had no idea what any of those things meant. Was brie a type of fish? Or a pasta? I was embarrassed to admit that I didn't know what she was talking about, but afraid to agree to split a meal I had never heard of, I told Liza that I didn't know what baked brie was. Or fig spread. Or crème brûlée.

Her jaw dropped. I saw both amusement and pity in her big brown eyes. I hated being looked at that way. She explained that brie was a type of cheese, and that baked brie was a warm cheese dish wrapped in fresh bread. She compared fig spread to jam and swore that it would complement the brie. She said that the crème brûlée was a vanilla sweet custard with a crunchy exterior made from caramelized sugar.

I agreed to split Liza's meal and put my Ramen back on the shelf. She grinned as we stood together in the checkout line. She insisted that I wouldn't regret my decision. I wondered where she had learned about such fancy sounding foods, and if the other girls knew anything about brie cheese or crème brûlée.

After the other girls finished making their purchases we headed back to the old nunnery, where we all made our way to the kitchen. The kitchen was much too small to hold all six of us comfortably, but we all found space.

I watched as Liza wrapped fresh dough around a large block of cheese, and when she finished, she placed it in the oven. The timer went off ten minutes later and she removed the cheesy bread from the oven and dusted it with the fig spread.

Placed next to the bottle of wine, it looked like a *Top Chef* entry. When I finally took a bite of the fancy baked brie cheese masterpiece, my eyes grew wide. I had never tasted anything like brie or fig before and I couldn't believe how much I enjoyed it. I took another bite. And another. I finished the small plate in front of me in just a few bites, then reached for seconds. Liza laughed as she watched me.

Liza explained that brie was a staple in her house. She and her family regularly indulged in charcuterie boards decorated with cheeses and meats. One of other girls in the kitchen explained that fine cheeses were a must in her house growing up too. Her mom was Italian and her dad was French, and they had both grown up eating lots of brie.

I ate baked brie and listened as the other girls in the kitchen continued to compare ancestry and culinary customs. Another girl chimed in about her family origins and cheese related traditions. Both of her parents had German ancestry, but they didn't really eat German food in her house. Their cheeses of choice were goat's milk and burrata. I had never heard of those cheeses either.

"Where's your family from?" one girl finally asked me. I was surprised. Growing up around mostly White people, I was usually prepared for awkward race-related questions. I had answers prepared for most of them. No, I don't wash my hair every day. Yes, my brown skin burns in the sun. But this time, I was so into the conversation and the plate of baked brie in front of me that I let my guard down.

I told the girls that my mom's family was from Haiti. Most Haitian people came from Africa, but it was hard to trace back their roots because they were brought to the island as slaves. My dad's ancestors were also brought to the United States from Africa as slaves. I didn't know where in Africa they came from either.

Moments ago, the kitchen had been full of joy and laughter, but now everyone sat quietly. I had committed the ultimate party foul. I had said "slave" at the dinner table. I knew from experience that White people hated talking about slavery. I looked around the small wooden table and was met with pity filled eyes.

"I'm so sorry," Liza said, as if she was personally responsible for capturing and enslaving my family. As far I was concerned, Liza had nothing to be sorry about. She had just made me the best and only baked brie I had ever tasted.

I couldn't attribute any of the customs in my present life to my ancestors. I didn't know what language my ancestors spoke, or what types of foods they ate. Liza said she couldn't imagine how hard it must be not knowing where in Africa my family came from.

I had never really spent time thinking about my ancestry before, but the way Liza looked at me now made me feel sorry for myself. Africa is a huge continent with many different cultures, languages, and people groups. Most Black people in the United States have no clue where in Africa they come from, and I was no exception.

I thanked Liza for her concerns and explained that although I didn't know much about my African roots, I was African American, and that was its own culture. Haiti had its own culture, too. I also had family traditions, like eating Ramen noodles.

Liza smiled and said she would join me in eating Ramen noodles the following evening if I wanted. I smiled back. Ramen may have felt like home, but I was more than happy to be eating baked brie.

CHAPTER 43
BAD HABITS

    I was venting to my therapist Carrie about how anxious I was feeling in a therapy session one evening when she asked me about my eating habits. I admitted that I didn't have much of an appetite and had lost five pounds in the last month. Carrie asked me if my weight often fluctuated when I was anxious, and I told her it did.
    Since I was a child, my emotions have always had a direct effect on my appetite. I didn't eat much when I was sad, stressed, angry, or anxious. Those tendencies followed me into adulthood. I lost ten pounds in law school and barely ate anything the week before the bar exam. I also had a hard time eating after breakups or disagreements with friends.
    Carrie jotted down notes as I told her about my history with food. She was adamant that I make proper eating a priority. I was already naturally small and couldn't afford to lose any weight. She cautioned that what we eat can influence how we're feeling, and if I didn't eat enough food, I wouldn't have the energy I needed.
    Carrie recommended I eat foods like bananas, oatmeal,

almonds, avocados, beans, and sweet potatoes to sustain me throughout the day. She also recommended that I start a food journal. She didn't want me to count daily calories or sugar intake, she wanted me to simply jot down what I was eating, and when. She thought it might help me be more intentional about when and what I ate. I was skeptical that writing down my meals would be helpful in any way, but I agreed to give it a try.

I started jotting down my meals in my journal the next day. Documenting my meals was much more emotionally taxing than I had anticipated. Forcing myself to write down everything I ate didn't just force me to come to terms with how often I was eating, but how poorly I was eating. Here are the meals I consumed in the first five days:

Day One: Pop tarts. Nachos.
Day Two: Ramen Noodles. Grilled Cheese. Cheetos.
Day Three: Cereal. Pizza.
Day Four: Instant Oatmeal. McDonald's Cheeseburger.
Day Five: Cereal. Taco Bell.

It was easy for me to ignore my eating habits when I was moving quickly through my days but writing down what I ate in my journal forced me to pay attention. I didn't eat much, but when I did eat, it was cheap junk food. As a kid, I had an excuse. My family didn't have any money, and food with low nutritional value like McDonald's and Ramen noodles were cheap and filling. But as an attorney making six figures, I had no excuse.

I quickly realized that my attachment to junk food was psychological. I didn't eat when I was hungry, or at certain times of the day. I ate when I was experiencing hard emotions. I looked forward to stuffing my face with pop tarts or Taco Bell. It reminded me of my childhood and made me feel safe. It gave me something to be excited about and distracted me from my anxiety. Or my anger. Or my despair. Or my boredom. On the days my emotions were too strong, and I let them consume me, I ate nothing at all.

I believe that because Black Americans have endured so much pain and trauma, we've learned to depend on food as one of our few sources of joy. Although my drug of choice for a long time was junk food, many Black people have an attachment to soul food. The concept of "soul food", ethnic cuisine traditionally prepared and eaten by Black Americans, originated during slavery. Black slaves were often fed undesirable cuts of meat, like chitlins (or hog intestines), pig feet, chicken liver, ham hocks, and fatback, as well as other leftovers from their southern masters. Some masters allowed their slaves to grow vegetables for themselves, like cabbage and collard greens.

Inspired both by African culture and traditional southern cuisine, over time the repertoire of soul foods expanded. Fried chicken. Macaroni and cheese. Sweet potato pie. Although incredibly delicious, foods like fried chicken, macaroni and cheese, and sweet potato pie, like my junk food diet, can be exceptionally high in saturated fat, cholesterol, salt, and sugar.

Determined to turn my own eating habits around, I started to do some research. I googled healthy snacks and easy dinner recopies. I was too busy most weekdays to cook anything elaborate, but there were lots of healthy recipes in cookbooks and online with low preparation times.

I started slow. First, I focused on establishing a routine. I tried to eat breakfast, lunch, and dinner every day. I incorporated fruit and vegetable smoothies into my diet, and I stocked my refrigerator with healthy snacks like hummus and Greek yogurt. I also learned how to make simple meals like pasta, baked chicken, and cauliflower rice. I ate junk food when I craved it, but I was careful to consume it in moderation. I was surprised to learn that with the right seasoning and preparation, healthy food could also taste good.

Fueling my body with foods that were good for me was an

act of self-care. Over time, I gained back all the weight I had lost. Carrie was right. Changing my diet influenced more than just my weight and appearance. I felt better and I had more energy. I stopped using food to distract myself from my emotions and started dealing with them instead. When I was anxious, I practiced deep breathing. When I was sad, I let myself cry. When I was bored, I found something productive to do.

I still allow myself to enjoy all the food that I love, but I try my best to make less emotion-based decisions and more health-conscious decisions about the foods I put in my body. I only have one body, and I know the types of foods I choose to eat can either work for me or against me. Sometimes, that means choosing what is good for me instead of what tastes or feels good to me.

PART 14
MO' MONEY

I loved my kindergarten teacher, Ms. Lowery, and according to my parents, she loved me too. She even offered to keep me for the summer. She told my parents that I was a joy to have in class, and if it would be helpful, she would be more than happy to let me stay with her for a few months. My parents immediately thanked her for her kindness but told her that would not be necessary.

Back then I was honored that my sweet White teacher wanted me to spend the summer with her and I didn't understand why my parents rejected her generous invitation so quickly. However, as an adult I can understand why her offering to take their child away may have felt more like an insult than a kind gesture.

I wondered whether Ms. Lowery offered to look after me simply because I was poor, or because I was poor and Black. I wonder if she looked at my poor Black parents and assumed they'd never be able to provide for me the way she could. I wonder if she worried that I'd grow up and continue the cycle of poverty.

But Ms. Lowery didn't know my parents. Although they both came from poor families, they were determined to set themselves and future generations up for financial success. I'm so thankful that I had a front seat to their process. From them, I learned how to hustle. I learned how to think about money strategically and how to make a little go a long way.

I also learned the difference between having money and being wealthy. Money will get you in the room, but wealthy people own the room. True wealth is not built in just one generation. It's prepped, planted, and cultivated. My parents have worked their way into rooms many people could never dream of but they're still fighting to own a room of their own. They've laid the foundation for my siblings and me to build wealth for our children and our children's children, one financial brick at a time.

CHAPTER 44
RICH DAD, POOR DAD

"It's too early," I groaned as I pulled the covers over my head. Getting out of bed before sunrise was the last thing I wanted to do during my Spring Break, but my mom was unrelenting. She was an early riser and had much more energy than I did. She pulled the covers back down and shoved a book in my face.

She pounced on the edge of my bed and insisted she needed to read me something. I squinted to read the cover of the book in her hands. It was too early for reading. Mom grinned as she read me the title on the front of the book, *Rich Dad, Poor Dad: What the Rich Teach Their Kids About Money–That the Poor and the Middle Class Do Not!*

I told Mom that it sounded like a great book, but I was too tired to listen to her talk. I suggested we talk about the book later, but she didn't want to read it to me later. She was excited to read it to me right then. Before I could respond, she opened the book and began to read.

"I had two fathers, a rich one and a poor one."

I knew that nothing I said was going to change her mind,

so I gave up and allowed her to continue reading.

At the beginning of his now popular book, Robert T. Kiyosaki explores the differences between the two influential father figures he had growing up. His biological dad believed that getting good grades and earning an education were the ultimate pathways to success. Although these sounded like positive ideals, Robert observed that his biological Dad did not do very well financially. He often struggled to save money and accepted the fact that he would never be rich. This is the dad Robert referred to as "Poor Dad."

Rich Dad, on the other hand, was the father of one of Robert's best friends and a close mentor to Robert. Like his biological father Rich Dad had a strong work ethic, but Rich Dad took a completely different strategy to building wealth. Instead of simply working for money, he believed it was important to learn how to make money work for him. He saw money as power. Despite dropping out of school in the eighth grade Rich Dad was a millionaire.

The more Mom read the more fascinated I became. The book explained the concept of passive income or learning to make money without having to actively work for it. In the book, Robert advocated for an updated perspective on wealth building strategies. I had never heard anyone use terms like "passive income", "financial literacy", or "wealth building" before.

When the sound of my growling stomach finally drowned out the sound of Mom's voice, I suggested that we take a break to eat breakfast. Mom laughed at this. It was already 1:00 p.m. and well past breakfast. I had been so engrossed in Robert's story that I hadn't even noticed six hours had passed.

Despite my initial early morning push back, I was hooked, and I wanted to know more. My mind raced with possibilities. What could I do now to start making passive income? How would I know whether my investments would be assets or liabilities? If I started my own business one day, would it be a standard corporation or an LLC?

When I was a young child, my family didn't talk about money often because we didn't have any. In fact, we didn't have much of anything. My first crib was a drawer pulled out from an old drawer padded with blankets. The only thing my parents owned was a small, shared Ford Escort.

However, by the time I turned sixteen my parents were in the top 10 percent of earners in the United States. We had more money than any of the other Black families I knew. All of a sudden, my parents were introduced to the world of real estate, stocks, investments, and life insurance. This drastic change in their financial situation prompted them to learn as much about money as they could.

My parents understood that building true generational wealth was going to take much more than just making money. It was going to require all of us to have a deeper understanding of how money works. They made it a point to teach me and my younger siblings Johnathan and Nia everything they could about wealth building.

Rich Dad, Poor Dad was just the first of many financial literacy lessons. Mom took me with her to seminars on how to make money from investing in real estate. We had open and honest conversations at the family dinner table about credit cards, loans, bills, and other financial stressors. When they earned bonuses or made money from their investments, they told us. When we couldn't afford something, they let us know that too.

Despite all their success and accomplishments, my parents could not afford to pay either for my undergraduate college or my law school education. Like many other newly affluent Black parents they were still paying off their own student loans by the time I applied for college. Although they couldn't afford to pay for my education, I'm so grateful I had parents who introduced me to the concept of financial literacy at a relatively young age. However, I would soon find out that there is no more valuable teacher than life itself.

CHAPTER 45
MONOPOLY MONEY

Legally Blonde, one of my all-time favorite movies, is about a beautiful blonde sorority girl from a well-off family named Elle Woods who went to law school to win back her ex-boyfriend. There's a line in the movie where in reference to Elle, one character asks, "Do you think she just woke up one day and said, 'I think I'll go to law school today'?" Although I did not go to law school to win back an ex-boyfriend, like Elle I decided to go to law school without thinking too deeply about it.

Law school just made sense since my dad was a lawyer. On top of that, I was smart, and I liked to argue. I knew that law school would be expensive, but never having worked a real job, I didn't fully appreciate the value of a dollar. Or in my case, hundreds of thousands of dollars.

Taking out a loan for law school felt a lot like playing monopoly. I spent lots of what felt like imaginary money and hoped my investments would eventually pay off. However, in real life you can't just clear the board at the end of the game, and as I quickly found out, the money I spent was not imaginary. The money I borrowed for law school was real, and I had to find a way to pay it all back.

I remember my law school exit loan counseling like it was yesterday. I sat in a small cold office across from a woman whom I'd never met before. She slid a stack of papers across the desk, and I didn't hear anything that came out of her mouth after that because my mind was fixated on the very large number written on the sheet of paper in front of me. According to that piece of paper, I now owed the government over $200,000 in student loans.

The number was much higher than I expected. My throat felt like it was constricting. "I'm sorry, I'm a little bit confused," I said when I could finally collect my thoughts well enough to form a coherent sentence.

The woman across the desk seemed unbothered by the look of panic plastered across my face. She calmly explained that the high number was probably because of the accumulating interest, and she showed me exactly where to look in the large stack of papers to see my current interest rate. I wondered how many times she'd had this conversation before.

I took a deep breath attempting to regulate my now racing heartbeat. I hadn't even found a job yet. Over the past few years I had spent so much time preparing for class, studying for exams, and looking for jobs that I hadn't taken a moment to even think about repaying my student loans. In fact, I hadn't thought about my loans at all since the day I applied for financial aid years prior. How would I ever pay that much money back? What would happen if I couldn't pay it back?

Higher education is more expensive than it ever has been. According to the Federal Student Aid report and the Federal Reserve Bank of New York report on total household debt, at the end of the second quarter of 2021 student loan debt stood at $1.59 trillion. For context, that's about double the total U.S. credit card debt of $790 billion.

Based on data drawn from ten national institutes and

organizations, a report in May 2021 showed that the average student loan debt for a bachelor's degree student was $29,000, but the average graduate degree student debt was $71,000, and could be multiples of this average depending on the graduate degree program. For example, the average student loan debt for a law school graduate was $145,000, for a medical school graduate $201,000, and for a dental school graduate $201,000. With aggressive student loan interest rates, many students owe more money years after graduating than they did when they graduated.

The debt crisis gets even more complicated for Black students. In June of 2020, Business Insider reported that 86.6 percent of Black college students take out federal loans to attend four-year colleges, compared to just 59.9 percent of White students. To make matters worse, the Economic Policy Institute reported that Black workers with advanced degrees were paid 14.9 percent less in 2019 than White workers with similar qualifications. With less money available to pay back higher student loan debts, the wealth gap between Black and White Americans continues to increase.

I've dealt with the paradox of this predicament for years. As soon as I open my mouth to complain about the amount of debt I've accrued, there's usually an older White person who tells me that I have no reason to complain because no one forced me to go to school. They tell me stories about how they worked their way through school and managed to do it without anyone's help.

All that sounds great in theory, but data compiled by the Education Data Initiative shows that after adjusting for inflation through 2020, the average student loan debt increased from $7,170 in 1970 to $30,000 in 2020, an increase of 418 percent. Working your way through college was much easier to do when the cost of college wasn't the price of a small island.

It also fails to acknowledge the relationship between

cultural capital and the politics of respectability as it relates to Black people. Both historically and in my experience, White people in America often require far less cultural capital than Black people to earn the same amount of respect. Earning a degree from a prestigious university is one of the few ways that Black youth can acquire lots of cultural capital quickly.

The vast differences between former President Barack Obama and former President Donald Trump show this principle. Barack Obama has two Ivy League degrees. He graduated from Columbia University with his bachelor's degree and from Harvard Law School, where he was president of the Harvard Law Review. Despite his academic accolades, White people across the nation who had far less education questioned Obama's intelligence and credentials. People demanded to see copies of his report cards and academic records in their attempts to undermine his ability to serve as President of the United States.

On the other hand, Donald Trump graduated from the University of Pennsylvania's Wharton School of Finance and Commerce with a bachelor's degree in economics without any academic honors or distinctions. Unlike Obama, Trump doesn't have a legal or any other advanced degree, nor did he have any political experience under his belt for that matter. Nonetheless, both Obama and Trump served as President of the United States.

As a Black woman, I believed that outside of the one in a million chance I became the next Oprah, my best shot at wealth was tied to cultural capital by means of higher education. UVA law was a top ten law school. With a degree of that caliber, I would have no trouble finding a good job.

What I failed to consider in my calculation was how far back my student loans would set me financially. Seven years post law school graduation, I now owe the government even more than I did when I graduated thanks to inflation and astronomical interest rates. Nonetheless, I don't regret my decision to go to law school. I do wish, however, that I had been more financially informed. I also wish that I had felt free enough to choose an alternate career path or a less expensive school without worrying about having to impress White people.

CHAPTER 46
RICH LAWYER, POOR LAWYER

"I need a raise," my coworker Danielle complained before taking a sip of her latte. Danielle was short and pale with long chestnut brown hair. She wasn't the most social person in the talent agency where we both worked, but we had always had great conversations and I enjoyed chatting with her during coffee breaks.

I told Danielle that I needed a raise too. I found out earlier that week that my landlord was going to increase my rent by $150 a month. Danielle shook her head back and forth. She and her boyfriend had just moved into a new apartment closer to our West Hollywood office, and her rent was much higher than it had been at her old place

I continued to complain about how expensive it was to be an adult. Therapy cost me $125 per session, I owed the DMV $400 for my car registration, and my one-year discounted Spectrum trial was about to run out. Between my rent, my bills, and my student loans, I was barely getting by. I shared with Danielle that I had thought going to law school was supposed to ensure that I didn't have to worry about money, but so far that hadn't been the case.

Feeling a shift in Danielle's energy as I talked about my finances, I changed the subject and asked her how her weekend was. At this she smiled and responded that she'd had a great weekend. She and her boyfriend had finished decorating their new apartment and celebrated over a glass of wine. She thought he was going to propose soon. She shared with me that although she was excited at the thought of getting engaged, the idea of planning a wedding stressed her out.

I empathized with Danielle. Weddings were increasingly becoming more expensive. I told her one of my friends spent over $100,000 on her wedding the previous year. That was almost half the amount of money I owed in student loans. I couldn't believe she had spent so much money for just one day.

"Wow," Danielle responded.

Had I paid more attention to the lack of enthusiasm in her voice, I probably would have ended the conversation there, but I didn't. I kept going. I told her that if I had that much money, the last thing I'd do was spend it on a wedding. To me, it was a stereotypical display of privilege. It was more money than most American families made in a year.

I asked Danielle how she and her boyfriend planned to pay for their wedding. Reluctantly, Danielle admitted that her family would pay for everything. I was intrigued. I asked her if her parents had given her a budget. She explained that she had a budget, but it wasn't one her parents set.

Danielle must have sensed my confusion about her vague response, because without me having to ask she offered an explanation. Her recently deceased grandmother had set aside money for Danielle's future wedding before she passed. Danielle wasn't allowed to touch the money until she got engaged.

This concept made logical sense, but it was one that was completely foreign to me. I had never known anyone who died and left behind money for things like their grandchildren's future weddings. I had only seen things like that happen in movies. If anything, all the old people I knew were in debt when they died, leaving their surviving family members and benefactors with nothing.

I conveyed to Danielle my condolences about her grandmother. The politically correct thing to do would have been to stop there, but I was intrigued. I wanted to know more about her "treasure chest." I assured her that she didn't have to answer if she didn't feel comfortable, but I was curious to know how much money her grandmother left her.

She giggled and said she didn't mind answering my question, but she just didn't want me to judge her. After hearing me talking about my other friend's extravagant wedding, I understood her reservation. I promised Danielle that I wouldn't judge her. If anything, I was jealous.

Danielle shared with me that her grandmother had left her $100,000 for her wedding. Her grandmother came from money. In addition, she had also paid for Danielle's law school tuition.

At that moment I realized how different Danielle and I were. We had both come from upper-middle-class families, and we had both graduated from great law schools, but while I was working hard to climb out of a financial hole, she was building on a foundation of wealth that had been laid before she was even born. My family had only just begun making money, but her family had accumulated wealth over generations.

Rich lawyer. Poor lawyer.

"I have one more question," I said to Danielle. I asked her why she needed a raise. Her wedding was paid for, she was making more than enough money to pay all of her bills, and she didn't have any loans or debts to pay off.

Danielle giggled again. I assumed she was amused by my curiosity. She said that she didn't need the money, but that she knew she deserved it. She was hardworking, and an asset to our company, "I know my worth," she said. I let that sink in.

CHAPTER 47
KNOW YOUR WORTH

There's a line from the movie *ATL* where one of the main characters, in an attempt to impress upon his female love interest how wealthy she is, shouts, "You got Picasso in yo' house!"

Pablo Picasso was a Spanish painter considered to be one of the greatest and most influential artists of the twentieth century. He is most associated with pioneering Cubism, a revolutionary new approach to representing reality more abstractly. Today, owning a Picasso painting is a symbol of success and class.

I remember learning about Picasso from my third-grade teacher, Ms. Martin, who was a kind, intelligent woman with a passion for life. She was a connoisseur of art, opera music, and fine dining. Every now and then she'd play music by the famous Italian opera singer Andrea Bocelli and allow the students to dance interpretively around the classroom.

Because of Ms. Martin, I gained an appreciation for what is considered high culture, or cultural objects of intellectual, philosophical, aesthetic, and artistic value, which a society collectively esteems as high value. Like Ms. Martin I gained an appreciation for Picasso's art. I loved how bold and imaginative his work was. As I learned more about him later in life, I became inspired not just by Picasso's art, but by his tenacity and his confidence. One evening, while falling down a rabbit hole on the internet reading about Picasso's impact on modern culture, I came across a story that taught me to never undervalue what I have to offer.

According to the story, Pablo Picasso was enjoying a nice meal alone at a café when a fan noticed him from across the room. The fan asked Picasso, who by then had gained quite a bit of notoriety for his art, to sketch something on a napkin for her. Picasso graciously agreed and sketched a small drawing on the napkin.

Before handing the woman the napkin, Picasso asked her for $100,000. Seeing that the drawing hadn't taken him much time to sketch, the woman was outraged. She refused to pay Picasso for the napkin since it had only taken a few seconds to draw.

Picasso then crumpled up the napkin, put it in his pocket and replied, "It took me forty years."

While there is debate about whether this story is really true, the moral of the story is clear. We are the ones who ultimately get to decide what we're worth. We can walk away from bosses who take us for granted, or from opportunities that offer to pay us much less than we believe we deserve. We are co-creators with God with full control over what we choose to believe and accept.

As Black people we have been made to believe that we are not worthy of success, and even when we achieve success many of us struggle with *imposter syndrome*, an inability to internalize the belief that we are deserving of our successes. This is not surprising given the historical mistreatment of Black Americans.

Today, Black people in America still continue to struggle

economically in comparison to White Americans, and earn less money than White Americans for doing the same jobs. According to the 2019 Federal Reserve's Survey of Consumer Finances, at $188,200, the median net worth of a typical White family was nearly eight times greater than that of a typical Black family, which had a median net worth of $24,100. The growing wealth gap between Black and White families perpetuates the idea that Black people are not deserving of wealth anywhere near that of White people.

When I first entered the workforce, the idea that I was not as deserving of wealth as my White counterparts governed all of my professional decisions and interactions. I was afraid to negotiate my salaries in fear of losing opportunities. I thought it better to seize an opportunity than lose it fighting for more money. Every time I learned that my White colleagues were earning more money than I was I grew angry.

Eventually, my anger inspired me to fight for myself. Now I pride myself on being able to accurately assess and advocate for my financial worth. When opportunities arise that don't offer adequate compensation, I turn them down.

My friends and I often joke that now when we walk into rooms, we set our intentions to carry ourselves with the same amount of confidence as the average White man. Instead of telling myself that I don't belong I tell myself that I am the most powerful being in the room, deserving of every good thing that this world has to offer. I had to learn to believe in my own ability to accumulate wealth with the same level of confidence that Picasso had when he asked the stranger at the restaurant to pay him $100,000 for a doodle on a napkin.

PART 15
A THOUSAND LITTLE THINGS

In America, White has always been considered the status quo. Everything else is considered "other." Movies with White actors and actresses are just considered movies, but movies featuring Black people are referred to as "Black movies." Flesh toned Band-Aids are made to match White skin. Public school history books are written by White people and are filled with stories about White people.

I recently found a short chapter book I wrote in the second grade called "Guilty". I wrote the book on lined notebook paper stapled together between two pieces of construction paper. On each page, I drew colorful illustrations to accompany the text.

The book was about a little girl whose younger brother caused conflicts around the house but blamed his older sister for them. I was the main character in my book. While casually flipping through it I was shocked to find that I had drawn myself as White in all the illustrations. The character labeled "me" had peach skin, a small pointy nose, and long, straight black hair. I had been so used to seeing White characters in stories that I couldn't write a Black character into my own story.

In his book *Long Walk to Freedom* Nelson Mandela said it was not one big thing but thousands of little things that had contributed to his lifelong fight for social justice:

> *I had no epiphany, no singular revelation, no moment of truth, but a steady accumulation of a thousand slights, a thousand indignities and a thousand unremembered moments produced in me an anger, a rebelliousness, a desire to fight the system that imprisoned my people. There was no particular day on which I said, Henceforth I will devote myself to the liberation of my people; instead, I simply found myself doing so, and could not do otherwise.*

Second grade was not the only time in my life I've wished I could be White. Like Nelson Mandela I have accumulated thousands of experiences over the course of my life that have led me to feel invisible, inferior, or inadequate as a Black woman in America. Some of them are vivid recollections while others feel like distant memories, colored less by what was said or done but more by how I felt in the moment. Together these experiences have contributed to my racial trauma.

The collective racial trauma of Black Americans is often glossed over by White America. Our stories are ignored, our experiences are discounted, and our pain is written off. In order to adequately address America's race problem, it's important for White people to consider the injustices and inequalities suffered by Black people not just on a macro level but in our daily lives. They must view the Black experience not just through the lens of slavery or Jim Crow, but through the lens of the thousands of race-based slights and indignities we experience on an everyday basis.

CHAPTER 48
SMART FOR A COLORED GIRL

I've been called "colored" two times in my life. The first time was by Professor Higgins, my Torts professor in my first year of law school. Professor Higgins was an old man with a southern accent and a head full of gray hair. His pale skin was wrinkly like a raisin, and he wore a similar version of a basic gray suit almost every day.

Professor Higgins was born in 1928. He grew up in an era of segregation where Black people and White people attended different schools and drank from separate water fountains. Sometimes he walked so slowly it almost looked like he wasn't moving at all. His hand shook whenever he wrote on the blackboard, and he wrote even more slowly than he walked. His class was one of the few in which I didn't struggle to take notes.

In class, Professor Higgins often referred to Black people as colored. I was one of only two Black people in our class of approximately thirty students. Whenever he used the word colored, people stared in my direction. I felt like an elementary school student sitting in an all-White class learning about slavery all over again. I don't think any of us knew how to respond, so instead, we all said nothing.

Once Professor Higgins told a story about the first time he'd seen a colored attorney representing a client in court. To his surprise, the colored attorney conducted himself just like a White attorney would. He was competent, poised, and well spoken. Professor Higgins grinned as he recalled the memory and then winked in my direction. I was mortified.

One afternoon, I paid Professor Higgins a visit during his weekly office hours. He had given me a B on my midterm, and I wanted to know what I did wrong. I felt like I understood the material and deserved a better grade.

Professor Higgins was amused that I wasn't satisfied with my B. "You are very smart for a colored girl," he said, grinning the way he had done in class when he told the story about the competent colored attorney he'd witnessed in court several months earlier.

I smiled at this but cringed on the inside. I wasn't smart for a colored girl. I was just smart. I should have told him his back-handed compliment made me feel uncomfortable, but just the thought of explaining why his comment was inappropriate was emotionally exhausting. Given his age and his life experience, I thought it was unlikely he would understand why his comment was offensive.

Professor Higgins couldn't explain why he had given me a B instead of an A. He assured me that my midterm exam was well-written and said that had he graded it on a different day and at a different time he might have given me a better grade. However, when I asked him if he'd be willing to re-consider my midterm grade, he shook his head no. "We cannot change the past," he insisted. He passed away from natural causes less than two years later.

The second time someone called me colored was a few years later on a flight back home to Virginia. I had graduated from law school at that point and was working as an entertainment attorney in Los Angeles, California. My flight was a red-eye, and I was exhausted after working all day.

The older White man seated next to me on the airplane smelled like Macy's cologne and peppermint tea. He watched me closely as I squished my carry-on bag into the small and empty space over his head and settled into my seat. A few minutes into the flight the old White man asked me what I did for a living.

I wasn't in the mood for conversation, but I didn't want to be rude. I smiled and told him that I was an attorney. His ocean blue eyes widened.

"Wow," he said, unable take his eyes off of me. "I've never met a colored attorney before."

His piercing eye contact made me feel almost as uncomfortable as his comment did. I didn't have the energy to contest his use of the word colored, or to continue to the inevitable uncomfortable conversation. Instead, I smiled again and put on my headphones.

Just as I was falling asleep about twenty minutes later, I felt a tap on my shoulder. It was the old man. Slightly irritated, I took off my headphones and looked at him. He apologized for staring at me and said that he didn't mean to be awkward, but he was fascinated. He knew that Barack and Michelle Obama were attorneys, but he had never actually met a colored attorney in person. He kept saying that I "just didn't look like an attorney."

My initial attitude softened as he spoke. Something about his curiosity was endearing. I watched him as he took in my afro, my multi-colored floral jacket, and my bright pink tennis shoes. I didn't look like the attorneys I'd seen on television either. On television attorneys were old and wore boring suits. They didn't have tattoos, or nose piercings, or rock kinky Afros like me.

The old man on the plane and I ended up having a great

conversation about our careers, our families, and our favorite books. He told me about his life growing up. He had been raised in the mid-west in an all-White environment. He didn't meet a Black person until he served in the U.S. military as a young man, and to his knowledge he had only recently met a Jewish person.

Both Professor Higgins and the old White man on the plane made judgments about me based on the color of my skin, but in both cases I lacked the emotional energy to challenge their biases. As a Black person, I don't want to constantly carry the burden of having to correct and educate White people. In some cases, it's much less exhausting to answer to "colored" than it is to address the old, racially insensitive elephant in the room.

CHAPTER 49
THE BLACK BOILING POINT

The first big general labor strike in the United States occurred in Philadelphia in 1835. It began as an impromptu affair when a group of coal heavers went on strike, demanding a ten-hour day. At the time, the working hours for blue-collar workers were long, the pay was low, and they worked under the constant threat of imprisonment for minor debts.

Exhausted from their long hours and poor working conditions, the workers finally decided they'd had enough. Eventually the laborers in Philadelphia reached their "boiling point." This is the point at which a gradual buildup of pressure and resentment causes a change or shift to occur. It is the point at which a situation becomes intolerable. Within a week, nearly twenty thousand workers had joined the strike. By the end of June 1835, most of them were granted the working hours they requested.

From the Boston Tea Party to America's participation in World War II following the attack on Pearl Harbor, there have been many moments in our history where Americans have reached their boiling point. Our national boiling points have incited revolutions, riots, and even full-blown wars. But we have personal boiling points in our individual lives too. They cause us to yell at our kids, move out of our neighborhoods, quit our jobs, and break up with our romantic partners.

Like everyone else, Black people have boiling points. There is a limit to the amount of racism, discrimination, bias, mistreatment, and police brutality that we can or will tolerate before we're pushed into taking more drastic measures. In 2016, Black NFL player Colin Kaepernick reached a personal boiling point that led him to start a peaceful protest against police brutality by kneeling during the national anthem. In the same way that soldiers take a knee in front of other fallen soldier's graves, Kaepernick took a knee to make a stand for Black civil rights.

Many White Americans misinterpreted Kaepernick's peaceful protests as a sign of disrespect. He was booed, bullied, and boycotted by hordes of angry fans. He was portrayed in the media as being ungrateful and unpatriotic and was publicly condemned by several White fellow NFL players. Many of my White social media friends also publicly condemned Kaepernick for his activism. Reading their posts on social media made me feel like his decision to peacefully kneel bothered them more than the countless deaths of African Americans who died at the hands of police officers.

Four years later, in the summer of 2020, America watched as George Floyd was violently killed by a White police officer who pinned him to the ground with a knee to his neck. For many Black people, myself included, George Floyd was a boiling point. From Trayvon Martin to Eric Garner, we had witnessed too many young Black men lose their lives unjustifiably and without consequence.

For me, George Floyd's death wasn't just a boiling point. It was defining and traumatic moment in my life. His death confirmed one of my deepest fears, that to some White people, Black lives don't matter. I lost the patience I once had to tolerate

White entitlement and stopped going out of my way to keep White people from feeling uncomfortable.

Black Americans weren't the only ones affected by George Floyd's death. People of all races and nationalities took to the streets to protest. The protests were by and large peaceful, but in a handful of instances they turned into riots. Apparently, the few riots were a much better story than the many peaceful protests because the news media played footage of the same few riots nonstop for weeks.

While I'm not an advocate for violence, it's important to pay attention to the underlying reasons why Black people in America may have felt the need to riot in the first place. White Americans have never willingly given up their privileges in the absence of a boiling point. It took an entire Civil War to convince White Americans to give up their slaves, and countless Black people were lynched, beaten, and killed in the fight for civil rights.

When I was younger, my mom used to say that if you continuously poke a sleeping bear, you cannot be surprised when the bear wakes up and retaliates. From slave owners and overseers to police officers and politicians, White people have poked Black Americans for hundreds of years. But to the dismay of many White people, we are no longer sleeping. We are awake, and we have reached our collective boiling point.

CHAPTER 50
LETTER TO MY FIVE-YEAR-OLD SELF

Dear Five-Year-Old Me,

I'm writing to you from a future space and time. I'm some years older than you, and time has taught me several lessons that I want to share with you. I believe they will help you live a happier, more purpose-driven life.

You don't know me yet, but one day I will be your safest space. I won't ever replace the role of your parents in your life, but I will be the person you come to most often when you're looking for answers. You will trust me with your fears and tell me all the secrets you can't tell anyone else.

First, I want you to know how deeply you are loved. God loves you so much. Even when you feel like you're all alone, he is with you. You may not always feel like God is listening or working for your good but pray anyway. Pray even when you feel like you've come to the end of yourself. I believe that sometimes God is just giving you what you would give yourself if you knew what he knew.

I want you to look at yourself in the mirror every morning and tell yourself that you are not only loved but that you are beautiful, and I want you to believe it. Don't hide who God created you to be. Hold your head high and wear your Black skin with pride. You may not appreciate it now, but one day people will pay for lips, hips, and skin that looks like yours.

I want you to know that your voice matters just as much as anyone else's. Use it boldly and use it often. Know that you possess the same gifts and capabilities that you admire in others. Anything you desire in this world can be yours if you're willing to put in the work.

You are your own biggest cheerleader. Sometimes you will win, and no one will be around to clap for you. Learn to clap for yourself. Celebrate every win, even if it feels small or insignificant.

You will learn even more from your failures than from your wins, so clap for yourself when you fail too. Even though things won't always work out the way you want them to, try your best to appreciate your process. Process is the garden where all beautiful things grow.

The world can be a cruel place, but don't ever forget to lead with love. Your intellect and your wit will be your weapons, but your heart will be your north star. When you're feeling lost, trust your heart to lead you back to yourself.

Love is the most beautiful thing that anyone can experience in this life. You don't have to go looking for it, it will find you. Your only job is to tend to it. Water it with kindness, patience, and humility. If you stop working to keep it alive it will die.

Remember that you have no control over anything in this world but yourself. The sooner you accept this reality the better. To love someone, to truly love someone, is to allow them to come just as they are. Do not try to change them. If they truly love you, they won't try to change you either.

Be willing to suffer for things that you love, but remember that you don't have to light yourself on fire to keep anyone warm. You are the fire. You burn with passion, and joy, and hope. That is the light this world needs.

Never dim your light or shrink yourself to make anyone else feel more comfortable. You never have to apologize for taking up space. Everywhere you are, you are supposed to be. One day you will try to imagine a world without yourself in it, and you will cry. You will know then that you don't just exist. You belong.

"No" is a complete sentence, and you are allowed to say no at any time and to anyone. You can say no to jobs, to sex, to pastors, and to uncomfortable requests. "No" never requires an explanation.

There is no greater gift you can give the world than your story. You must fight to tell it no matter what. Not every piece of your story will unfold pleasantly, but all the unfolding will lead to growing, and growing is living. As we grow, we become more equipped to show up as healthier, more healed versions of ourselves. And the world benefits from that.

I want you to know that you can trust yourself. Your life belongs to you, and you get to decide how to live it. People will try to advise you at every turn, but no one knows you better than you know yourself. Trust your instincts, leap with conviction, and walk boldly through every door you choose to open.

I know that you worry. You worry that you won't figure it all out. But you don't have to have all the answers. You just have to keep asking yourself the right questions. One day, it will all settle in your soul. And you will smile.

ACKNOWLEDGMENTS

Writing this book has been the greatest honor of my life. It is not just the book itself, but the process, that I am eternally grateful for. Through this process, I've become more intimately acquainted with my inner child than I ever thought possible. Writing this book has come with its own specific set of challenges. I want to take a moment to acknowledge all the people who helped me get this book out of my physical body and into the world.

To my mother and father, Dr. Anastasia Williams and Sanford S. Williams, Esq., words can't express how much I love and respect you, not just as parents, but as friends. Thank you for making me feel like I could become anything in this world, and for teaching me to color outside the lines.

To my siblings Dr. Sanford Johnathan Scott Williams and Nia C.C. Williams, thank you for challenging me to become the best version of myself, and for supporting me in everything that I do. The big three for life!

To my goddaughter and niece Zoe, thank you for giving me a future to fight for.

To my grandparents, Dr. John Bayardelle, Claudia Bayardelle, Sanford Joseph Williams, and the late Constance Williams, and all my aunties, uncles, and cousins, thank you for showering me with love and affirmation. I feel so blessed to have a small piece of all of you in me.

To Michael Nelder Henderson III, thank you for being my mirror and my partner. Thank you for believing in me unconditionally, especially on the days when I didn't believe in myself, and for helping me bring my book baby into this world.

To Sheila Howard and Jackie Armstrong, I couldn't ask for better mentors. God brought the three of us together in the most incredible way, and I will always be grateful for the contributions you have made in my life.

To Nancy Redd, thank you for inspiring me to write this damn book on the days I felt defeated.

To Carla Santiago, thank you for listening to me, processing with me, and supporting every idea and every project I've ever had.

To my therapist Carrie, thank you for helping me find my way back to myself.

And last but not least, to my publisher, Benjamin Taylor, thank you for giving me an opportunity to tell my story. I can't imagine having gone through this process with anyone else.

KIARA IMANI

Kiara Imani is an attorney and co-host of *Don Amiche vs. Everybody + Crysta & Kiara*, a daytime talk show on Los Angeles radio station KBLA Talk 1580 AM. She is also the co-founder of LikeU Cards, a getting to know you card game that facilitates human connection and meaningful conversation. Kiara graduated from the University of Virginia School of Law and received her bachelor's degree from the University of Virginia with a major in political science. She has been featured in *Forbes*, *Oprah Magazine*, *The Huffington Post*, *Blavity*, and more. *Therapy Isn't Just For White People* is her debut memoir Connect with Kiara Imani on the web at kiaraimani.com, on Twitter @kiara_imani, and on instagram @kiaraimaniwill.